THE BREWERY AND ITS PEOPLE

CLARENCE "COOPEN" JOHNSON

FITGER'S PUBLISHING
Duluth, Minnesota

FITGER'S PUBLISHING
600 East Superior Street
Duluth, Minnesota 55802
www.fitgers.com

Fitger's: the brewery and its people

Text: Clarence "Coopen" Johnson and Scott Vesterstein
Additional research and text: Barbara Beerhalter Chapman
Project coordination: Tami Tanski-Sherman
Proofreading: Chris Godsey
Copy and content editing: Scott Pearson
Cover, end papers, and interior design and layout: Tony Dierckins

Contemporary photos by Jeff Frey and Associates.
Photos in chapter 18 by Jim Wood.
Photo on page 135 by Tony Dierckins.
Photo on page 53 courtesy Mrs. George Frost of Cromwell, Minnesota.

Historic photos, newspaper clippings, and brewery memorabilia courtesy
the Fitger's Museum, Clarence "Coopen" Johnson, and the Beerhalter family.

Incline Railway postcard on page 65 from *Greetings from Duluth, Volume 1* by Jerry Paulson,
Published by X-communication, Duluth, Minnesota. Used by permission.

Diagram on page 148 by Tony Dierckins, based on a hand-drawn original from the Fitger's archives.

05 06 07 08 09 • 5 4 3 2 1

Library of Congress Control Number: 2004115373

ISBN: 0-9753646-0-X (hardcover) & 0-9753646-1-8 (softcover)

Printed in Singapore by TWP America

Production assistance and publishing consultation by

www.x-communication.org

*For the early owners and employees of Fitger's Brewery
and the people who have continued
to uphold its traditions into the twenty-first century.*

*Special thanks to
Sally Anderson, Bob Greenly, Dave Hoops, George Hovland III,
Jason Humphreys, Rockne Johnson, Jim Makitalo, Tim Nelson, Nancy Shamblott,
the Fitger's-on-the-Lake LLC partners, and everyone else who helped make this book possible.*

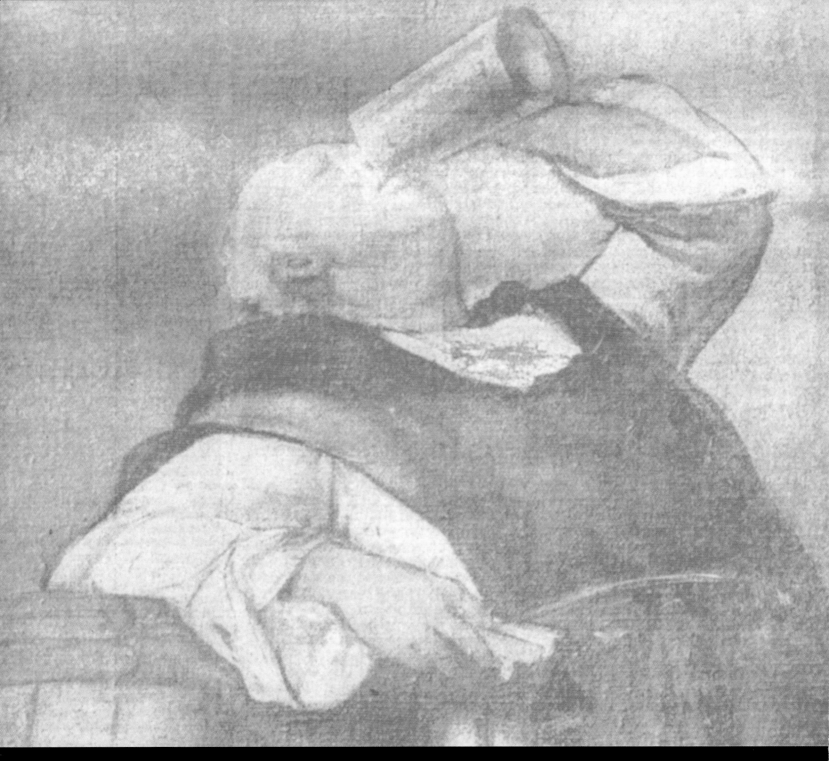

Photo of a sketch by Arthur Fitger which hangs today in the Fitger's boardroom, now part of Fitger's Inn.

CONTENTS

FOREWORD

In the late 1990s the Fitger's Brewery Complex began to host annual reunions for Fitger's past employees. During the reunions I always found myself talking to Clarence "Coopen" Johnson. He could weave a story and remember facts like no one else I have ever talked to—he was "the keeper of the story." After a couple of years, we got together and decided it was time to write a book about Fitger's and its people, to make sure these stories were kept for future generations to enjoy. Coopen had so much information from the past, including August Fitger's business journals, one-of-a-kind pictures, and many more items needed to make the book virtually complete. Without Coopen's help, this book never would have been published. We combined our efforts with Barb Beerhalter, whose great grandfather, John Beerhalter, had at one time been president of the brewery. Her family had also saved irreplaceable diaries and old pictures. We had all the pieces in place to give a historically accurate portrayal of Fitger's past—and ended up spending over three years cataloging the information and pictures. I have had a wonderful time working with Coopen, Barb, and also Tami Tanski-Sherman, the museum curator at Fitger's, to make this book a reality. We all hope you enjoy it.

— Scott Vesterstein
Owner, Fitger's Brewery Complex

Above, left to right, Clarence "Coopen" Johnson, Scott Vesterstein, and Barb Beerhalter.

Opposite: A wooden Fitger's beer keg.

INTRODUCTION

Most individuals have a special year that is an important milestone in their lives. Mine was 1948. In June, I married Nancy Cavanaugh after a seven-year romance that started in high school. Two weeks later, I accepted my first job at Fitger's Brewing Company. Little did I realize another romance was "brewing" that would also last more than fifty years—my fascination with the history of this famous landmark.

My initial interest in the brewery's history started early. My temporary job description called for working or filling in at any department of the beer making. Every Friday, I was scheduled to pick up all the burnable materials in the brewery complex and deposit them in the boiler house for burning. Much of the material originated from the brewery office. One Friday, I noticed the waste was heavier than usual. As I fed the material into the boiler bins, I noticed old office records dating back some fifty years. Why I kept some of those records, I do not know. But it did arouse my curiosity about the plant and thus started my personal interest in Fitger's history.

Every Friday thereafter, I would scrutinize the office waste. It would have been easier for me to ask an office employee to set aside such records, but this was a "no-no" during that era. No employee went to the office except on official business. The office staff was comprised of seven workers, not counting officers. When you visited the office, you could hear a pin drop. Discipline prevailed throughout the brewery.

In the early 1960s, business conditions didn't warrant the summer job I formerly held, so I applied for a job as a brewery guide, which involved morning and afternoon tours of the facilities. This job gave me a direct pipeline to Walter Johnson, the company vice-president. He was the only person with whom I talked who had known both August Fitger and his business partner, Percy Anneke. He had praise for both individuals. Both were gentlemen and very business-like, always keeping an arm's length from employees, except for key personnel. They were hardly ever together in the brewery. Both traveled for extended periods of time. Mr. Johnson was the plant historian, and he kept most records at his fingertips, e.g., when career employees started at the brewery, when they died, when the first truck was purchased, when the last horse was sold, and labor agreement provisions. I wish I had spent more time talking with him.

Later I became the Fitger salesman on the Iron Range for a period of two years. Shortly thereafter, new management took over the plant and made economic changes. I then assumed the city distributorship for Fitger's Beer. The "new management" was temporary until John Ferris became president of the brewery. I continued city deliveries until 1972 when the brewery discontinued brewing beer. Fitger's Brewery was 91 years old when it succumbed, the oldest manufacturing company in Duluth at the time.

I continued in the beer business by renting the bottle house and using it as a warehouse for beer trucked to Duluth from Schell's Brewery in New Ulm. They were a "contract" brewer. Schell's Brewery bottled, canned, and kegged Fitger's beer. This ended in 1984 when the brewery complex was sold. But during those twelve years, I also had the opportunity to read old brewery records and meet members of the Anneke and Fitger families to expand my knowledge.

Although my relationship with Carlo Anneke went back many years, I met Mrs. Victor Anneke and Victor

---

Opposite: The Fitger family coat of arms, a gift from the Fitger family to author Clarence "Coopen" Johnson for his involvement in keeping the Fitger family history alive in Duluth.

Anneke Jr. on only two occasions. I was surprised at their limited knowledge of the brewery. It was totally blank about the Fitger side of the story. But sometimes fate plays interesting cards.

In the mid-1970s, a great grandniece of August Fitger stopped in the office and left her address. This led to a correspondence with Fitger's grandniece and a visit to Kiel, Wisconsin, where she shared many pictures and other Fitger's memorabilia. Another strange occurrence came in the early 1980s—three people stopped by one evening when the brewery happened to be open because of a board meeting. The secretary took their names and the next day I had Mr. and Mrs. Bengt Fitger and their daughter over to my home.

Bengt was the grandson of August Fitger's brother Peter, who had moved to Sweden about the same time August had moved to the United States. He and his wife were visiting their daughter who was an exchange student across the bay in Superior, Wisconsin. Through them I began a correspondence with August's nephew in Bremen. I later visited the Fitgers in Sweden and Lothar Anneke in Germany. Then five years ago, a great granddaughter of August Fitger visited Duluth and I showed her the brewery and old pictures and later visited the Fitgers in California.

In retrospect, I can see how busy the lives of the Fitgers and Annekes have been. The brewery was just one phase, and to many of them not as important as other phases. I spent a lot of time on this project over the years. But I believe it was a worthwhile undertaking. And best of all, we ended up with an interesting story.

— Clarence "Coopen" Johnson,
2004

August Fitger kept a separate business journal for each year. Coopen Johnson was able to rescue most of them from the trash. Pictured are journals from 1925 and 1927.

PART I

The Nineteenth Century

The A. Fitger & Company's Lake Superior Brewery in 1891.

CHAPTER I

Legacy

Sidney Luce came to Duluth in 1857 and invested in land located in the nearby Portland town site, on what is now Seventh Avenue East. He hired Gottlieb Bush, a young bachelor, to help him build a brewery there, by a stream which became known as "Brewery Creek." The creek has kept that name since 1859.

In Walter Van Brunt's *History of Duluth and Saint Louis County*, Luce described how it all started: "There was nothing doing to relieve the stringency of the times. Our population was steadily decreasing and to retain what remained was a matter of anxiety. In canvassing the mat-ter, it was found there were four single men out of employment, one of them being a practical brewer. He suggested the building of a brewery as the four could do all of the construction and carry it on. As this seemed likely to add a little to our enlivenment, I encouraged the project by giving them the location and otherwise assist-ing. The enterprise was not a pecuniary success."

Luce worked hard to ensure the brewery's success but the depressed economy could not support it and he even-tually shut down the operation. Luce sold the brewery to Nicholas Decker in 1865.

Growing Pains

In 1855, the Treaty of La Pointe opened up land in Saint Louis, Lake, and Cook Counties, inspiring the building of many town sites along the North Shore of Lake Superior, including Duluth. From Fond du Lac to what is now Lester Park, eleven town sites were platted out for development, including street locations, in less than eighteen months.

Four of these town sites—Oneota, Fond du Lac, Duluth, and Portland—were vying to be the "City of Destiny." When the locks at Sault Sainte Marie opened, Duluth, at the head of the lakes, seemed to be the city that would become the great commerce site of the northland. Population on the Duluth side of the bay increased rapidly until railroad bond failures caused the Panic of 1857. In a few short months, the population dwindled from about three thousand people to fewer than a thousand.

In 1861, according to a map prepared by U.S. Army Engineer George Meade, there were only twelve houses in Duluth and seven in Portland. Of the few people still living in Duluth, several enlisted in the Union Army. Duluth's population remained at an all-time low until 1865 when gold fever hit on the Vermilion Range near Tower. A road was built from Duluth to the gold country with private funds, and for the first time in many years the few citizens remaining in Duluth felt optimistic about their futures.

Decker Purchases the Duluth Brewery

Decker had moved to Superior, Wisconsin, in the 1850s. In 1857 he moved to the Oneota town site along St. Louis Bay in what is now part of West Duluth (Spirit Valley). He later worked as a government farmer at Fond du Lac for a couple years and then moved to Eagle River, Michigan. When he finally returned to Duluth in 1866 and purchased the brewery, he built a boarding house, Vermillion House, adjacent to it. He hired Gottlieb Bush as his practical brewer.

Duluth's first newspaper was established in 1869 and Decker immediately used it to advertise. He placed two ads in the second issue of the *Duluth Minnesotian* on May 1, 1869. By that year, however, Decker no longer employed Gottlieb Bush nor anyone else. He was operating the brewery by himself and apparently there was some question about the quality of his beer. This soon changed, and on May 22, just three weeks after his first ad appeared, the *Minnesotian* reported, "Mr. Decker, at length, has employed a brewer, minding his public house as much as possible without having to make beer for the minions. We will now have first class beer all the time or there will be one brewer taking a bath in the big Lake Superior."

A New Railroad and a New Paper

In 1868, Jay Cooke decided that Duluth would be one of the terminal points of his future railroad, the Northern Pacific. Duluth then became known as Jay Cooke's town and many people from other parts of Minnesota and the adjacent states moved to Duluth anticipating an economic boom.

In 1869, the Portland Proprietors offered large parcels of land to Dr. Thomas P. Foster, a physician and newspaper editor, to come to Duluth and start its first newspaper, the *Duluth Minnesotian*. Foster coined the phrase, "The Zenith City of the Unsalted Seas," which the Duluth Chamber of Commerce used as a slogan well into the mid-1900s.

Next Decker started a saloon in downtown Duluth. The *Minnesotian* reported on July 10, 1869, "Mr. Decker purchased a property on Superior Street near the Hunter Building for the sale of his First Class Beer."

After the canal to Duluth Bay was built (see sidebar on page 4), Duluth began to boom, sometimes at the expense of Superior. Klein and Kiichli, two German immigrants, relocated their brewery from Superior to Duluth.

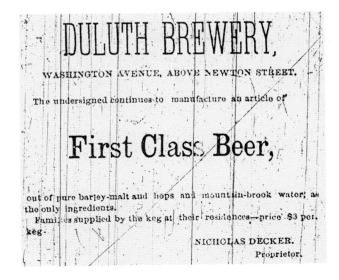

Left: The first Duluth Brewery ad in the Minnesotian. *The keg mentioned is actually a quarter barrel, which is about eight gallons. Above: Nicholas Decker also advertised his boarding house in the same issue of the paper.*

Life on the Frontier

In 1869, Duluth was still a frontier town comprised of professional people and single men, often transients who moved from town to town looking for jobs. These people frequented the saloons. A December 11 article in the *Minnesotian* noted, "The young man in Decker's Beer Saloon recently shot through the palm of his left hand while carelessly showing off his revolver is getting along nicely while under the judicious treatment of Dr. Cullum."

In August 1870 the first murder in Duluth occurred. Thomas Stokely, the son of the mayor of Philadelphia, was working on the construction of the Lake Superior Mississippi Railroad. According to the newspaper, he and his cohorts got into a drunken brawl and killed a Duluthian named George Northrup. Since Duluth did not have a courthouse or a jail, Stokely and his friends were kept under guard in the "cooler," a hand-dug cave in the side of the hill adjacent to the Duluth Brewery. The next day they were transferred under heavy guard to St. Paul, which had both a jail and a courthouse.

Duluth in 1869 (facing north from what is now Canal Park), the year ads for Nicholas Decker's Duluth Brewery first began to appear in the Duluth Minnesotian, *Duluth's first newspaper. Decker also owned a saloon and the Vermillion House Hotel, a boarding house.*

The *Tribune* newspaper, owned by R. C. Mitchell, also moved to Duluth from Superior. The Klein and Kiichli's brewery was located on Seventh Avenue West and Fourth Street on the banks of the sparkling Cascade Creek, which still trickles down near the foot of Mesaba Avenue. After a few years of operation, Decker bought the brewery and moved the equipment to his brewery at Brewery Creek.

In early January of 1875, Nicholas Decker passed away from consumption, a term used at the time for chronic lung diseases. He was buried in a cemetery on the western side of Chester Creek, which would be from Fourth Street to Seventh Street today. Most of the people buried in the Chester Creek Cemetery, excluding Decker,

were moved to the new Forest Hill Cemetery because it was believed that the cemetery was contaminating the creek and causing typhoid. Decker's body was moved to Calvary Cemetery.

Old Brewery Has New Problems

In 1877, Michael Fink leased the brewery from the Decker family. There were then eighteen saloons in Duluth, most of which did some business with the brewery. The brewery also had thirty private accounts that purchased beer.

Fink, a native of Tyrol, Germany, had originally immigrated to the Chaska area, southwest of Minneapolis, where his brother Conrad was a farmer. He later started

Digging a Canal

In late 1870, the Lake Superior Mississippi Railroad brought the first passenger train to Duluth. It arrived at its terminal point on the lakefront about where Fourth Avenue East is today. A wooden, rock-filled crib next to the dock extended into the lake. The dock was used to unload immigrants and other passengers coming to Duluth and to export grain from Duluth. Three Duluthians, Clinton Markell, Charles Graves, and Roger Munger, constructed Elevator A to be used for storing grain adjacent to the crib. The loading dock was unprotected from Lake Superior and was eventually demolished by continual pounding of waves generated by storms Duluthians know as "northeasters."

The following year, Duluth businessmen and laborers remedied this situation by cutting a canal through Minnesota Point to allow vessels to enter the safe harbor of Duluth Bay (now St. Louis Bay). Superior, which had a natural harbor, went to court in St. Paul and succeeded in getting an order for Duluth to stop work on its canal. Duluth volunteers learned of the coming order, mustered extra help, and continued digging through the night. They finished the canal before the messenger with the stop order could reach Duluth. Eventually, the canal was approved as a *fait accompli*, an accomplished fact.

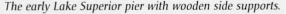

The early Lake Superior pier with wooden side supports.

the Stillwater (Minnesota) Brewery and was quite successful until he lost it due to unsuccessful investments in other ventures. Fink arrived in Duluth in 1873 at the age of thirty-three, but it is unclear what he did before leasing Decker's brewery four years later. By 1878, according to the Duluth newspaper, his personal property had dwindled to $323 and he paid $15.82 in personal property taxes, which still put him in the upper middle class.

The Decker Brewery, though only twenty years old, was in dire need of many repairs. A local newspaper reported, "The addition containing the beer cooler of Mr. Fink, in which was contained a hundred eighty kegs of beer, was undermined by Brewery Creek on Wednesday night, fell down, spilling the beer into the brook and wrecking the building. It is estimated that the loss to Mr. Fink is altogether about four hundred dollars. We warn good templars and blue ribbon folks not to go fishing in

From City to Village

The prosperity of the late 1860s and early 1870s, driven by Jay Cooke and his railroad, came to a grinding halt with the failure of the Northern Pacific Railroad. The entire country fell into an economic depression, called a "money panic" at the time. In 1873, the City of Duluth filed bankruptcy and reverted back to village status. The village limits were reduced to a span from Fourth Avenue West to the brewery on Seventh Avenue East.

Brewery Creek below the brewery as it would look suspicious, possibly a brook would start a bar at its mouth."

There was much speculation in the press and the village of Duluth as to what Fink would do after the destruction of the addition. Brewing did continue, and it

The M. Fink & Company–Lake Superior Brewery. The Brewery Saloon, predecessor to today's Pickwick, was on the right side of the building. Brewing facilities and offices were to the left. The second floor included employee sleeping quarters and storage rooms.

was reported in the newspaper on June 1, 1881, that Fink paid $300 to the government for federal keg stamps. This was enough to conclude that business was good. Prosperity was returning once again, and in 1881 Duluth's boundaries expanded to 14th Avenue East, 30th Avenue West and down Lake Avenue to the canal.

The Brewery on Superior Street

In May 1881, Fink announced that he would erect a substantial building on Superior Street. Construction of the new Lake Superior Brewery began September 19, 1881. This was big news for Duluth.

The newspaper reported, "Ground was yesterday broken for Alderman Fink's new brewery. The site is on Superior Street between Sixth and Seventh Avenue East. The building is to be seventy by seventy, three stories high and veneered with brick. The foundation is to be of stone. Louis Meining Senior has the contract for doing the excavating and furnishing the stone and sand for the foundation. Mr. Meining is an old hand at such business and Mr. Fink has done well to secure his services. Charles Yaeger will do the masonry work. Mr. Fink's intention is to put up a building that should be second to none in the state for the purpose intended and will furnish it with all the improvements known to modern breweries. The building is to be ready for occupancy about the middle of November. And to accomplish this, a large force of men will be put on

Both sides of an original Brewery Saloon beer token.

and the work of construction rushed forward with a whip." Forty-five days later, the newspaper dated November 4, 1881, noted, "Fink's new brewery looms up in mammoth shape, almost enclosed. Mr. Fink expects to have it running in a short time." Fink purchased the cream-colored brick for the exterior of his brewery from Wilhelm Schwartz, the owner of the Brainerd Steam Brick Yard.

The brewery was completed in 1882 and included offices, sleeping quarters for employees, all the facilities needed to brew beer, and its own drinking establishment called the Brewery Saloon. During this time, most breweries had their own bar where they would host parties, sometimes for free, as a gesture of goodwill to the community. Salesmen and other brewery officials would pass out beer tokens, sometimes called chips or coins, which were good for one free glass of beer. The M. Fink & Company–Lake Superior Brewery sold its first beer in August 1882. They sold only pony kegs at first, which are one eighth of a barrel, or about four gallons. All the beer was brewed in a kettle that held twenty-nine to thirty-two barrels and was heated by wood. That August, the brewery sold 2,501 pony kegs, which was considered a very good start.

Fink eventually sold beer as far west as Aitkin, Minnesota, and as far east as Port Arthur, Ontario (now Thunder Bay). The expansion was costly and there was new competition from breweries in Milwaukee, LaCrosse, and even the Twin Cities. Many breweries were featuring bottled beer, which was new to the industry. The costs of constructing the brewery and the expansion of territory cost Fink more than he originally anticipated. In November 1881, Fink had mortgaged several lots he owned in the Portland Addition to Isaac Hinckley of Philadelphia for $3,000 to help finance the construction of the brewery. Six months later he mortgaged two more lots to William Constance of Duluth for $2,000. Even though sales were strong, money was needed to keep up with the new competition and for a possible bottling operation, which was under consideration.

CHAPTER 2

The August Fitger Era Begins

While dealing with the deteriorating buildings of the old Decker Brewery, constructing the new brewery, and expanding the brewery territory, Fink also was the practical brewer. It had become too much responsibility for one man to handle, so on November 11, 1882, Fink hired a 28-year-old German by the name of August Fitger to work at the brewery. Fitger would be the first journeyman brewmaster to work in a Duluth brewery. Still single at the time, he rented a room near the brewery and focused on his work.

Less than six months after he was hired, Fitger purchased one half of the Lake Superior Brewery for $18,000. Actually, an agreement was reached among three people: August Fitger, Michael Fink, and Percy Anneke. Anneke was a Milwaukee friend of Fitger who believed the beer business would be a good investment opportunity. The agreement stipulated that Fitger would buy half the brewery, which he did in April 1883, and become partner with Fink. Anneke, who was taking care of his ailing mother in Milwaukee, would purchase the other half after his mother's demise in 1885. The Fitger-Anneke agreement was made with a handshake and not actually written and signed until 1892.

August Fitger, circa 1915.

New Brewery is Humming

In 1883, the first full year of operation, M. Fink & Company—Lake Superior Brewery sold 5,205 barrels, which was more than five times the sales a year earlier at the Decker Brewery. The Decker Brewery, under Fink, had hired only part-time employees. Fink now had a superintendent and brewmaster in Fitger and four other full-time employees. Their wages were anywhere from $45 to $51 a month. Two full-time employees, Joe Wargin and Andy Haller, lived on the second floor of the brewery. They paid $16 a month for their room and board. (It's interesting to note that Wargin's grandson Otto drove a beer truck at Fitger's in the 1960s and Haller's grandson worked at the brewery driving a beer truck and a pop truck into the 1960s as well.)

Brewing Families

August Fitger was born in 1854 in Delmenhorst, Germany, to Peter Dietrich Fitger, a hotel owner, farmer, and the town postmaster, and his wife, Clara. They had ten children, eight of whom survived infancy.

Fitger's siblings lived in countries throughout the world. His oldest brother, Arthur, lived his entire life in Bremen, Germany. Emil also moved to Bremen. Elfrieda, his sister, married Ferdinand Krieger and moved to Kiel, Wisconsin, outside Milwaukee. Robert moved to Moscow and became a businessman. Peter moved to Sweden and ventured into mining, farming, and other businesses.

August Fitger left Germany on October 20, 1871, when he was seventeen. The ship he traveled on, the *Christal*, was not a steamer but a sailing vessel; the passage took 64 days. The *Christal* carried more than 200 people bound for the United States. Fitger, who traveled first class, was the first person on the roster and was identified as a merchant. The ship arrived in New York City on Christmas Eve 1871. Fitger disembarked and headed to his sister's home in Kiel, Wisconsin.

Once Fitger established a base with his sister, he moved around the country for six or seven years working at various breweries in cities such as Cleveland, Milwaukee, and St. Louis. He also worked at a lumber company in upper Michigan and it was around that time that he went to school for business and bookkeeping. He eventually decided that he wanted to become involved in the brewery business and returned to Germany, entering the Weihenstephan Brewing School in Munich, which is still in business and advertises itself as the leading and oldest brewery in the world.

Once he finished school, he entered an apprenticeship at a brewery in Germany, eventually returning to the United States where he worked in several more breweries before Fink recruited him to Duluth.

During this time, people were moving west in large numbers in search of land and opportunity, creating a growing market for the brewery business. It was a good time for Fitger to start his legacy.

Percy Anneke was born in Milwaukee in 1850 to Fritz and Mathilde Anneke. His full name was Percy Shelley Anneke; his mother named him after the famous British poet. The Anneke family had fled to the United States following the unsuccessful German Revolution of 1848, during which Fritz had been briefly imprisoned for fighting against the monarchy. The Annekes had six children after moving to the States. Three died of diphtheria, leaving only Percy, Fritz Jr., and Hertha. The Annekes were in Europe when the American Civil War broke out. Fritz returned to the States to fight in the Union Army, but his family was stranded in Europe with insufficient funds to return home. Percy was educated in Paris and Zurich. In 1865, Mathilde and the children finally returned to the United States, where Percy finished his education. Before joining Fitger's he worked as an auditor at Joseph Schlitz Brewing Company and at the Second Ward Bank in Milwaukee.

With Fitger handling the brewing, Fink now had time to work on expanding his market. He opened accounts in the newly organized towns of Grand Rapids, Thompson, Agate Bay (later known as Two Harbors), NP Junction (which became Carlton), Vermilion on the Vermilion Range, and Tower.

Beer Delivery by Boat and Train

The expansion of territory created delivery problems for the company. Within the Duluth area, deliveries were made by horse-drawn wagon. However, many of the accounts in the surrounding area were not accessible by road and alternative methods of transportation had to be used.

In the 1880s, Agate Bay was a fast-growing town because there were plans to link the Vermilion Range with Agate Bay by railroad. Beer was delivered to Agate Bay by boat, where a teamster would pick up the beer and deliver it to the brewery's thirteen accounts. The brewery stocked

Percy Anneke, circa 1900.

Below: Fink & Company entered a horse-drawn float in the July 4th Parade in 1884. The woman in the window is the wife of Joe Wargin, a brewery worker. They lived on the second floor and had a child while they lived at the brewery. Their grandson Otto Wargin would drive truck for Fitger's into the 1960s.

The Brewery Saloon. Franz Heinrich (seated front center) was a close friend of Fink and managed the saloon from 1884 until his death in 1909.

a warehouse in Agate Bay to supply the saloons in the winter months; boat traffic became very dangerous during that time.

Once a week during the shipping months, Fink would board a boat for Agate Bay to visit his accounts and make

Fun with Salesmen

When a brewery salesman called on his accounts, it was expected that he would buy a round of his product to promote good relations. The salesman, of course, would have a bottle himself and remark how great his beer tasted. Many bartenders would dupe the salesman by switching bottle labels and serving the salesman his rival's beer.

collections. It was customary to spend money at the bars, so one had to be very disciplined to make it back to Duluth sober. Other areas, such as NP Junction, Thompson, and Cloquet, were accessible by railroad. Beer was loaded with the Lake Superior Mississippi Railroad at the depot located on Fourth Avenue East and the lakefront. Fink also visited these accounts once a week, riding the railroad.

The brewery delivered beer two ways to the thirty-three accounts located in the Superior, Wisconsin, area. During the shipping season, beer would be delivered to lakeside docks in the Garfield area. It was then delivered by boat to Superior and transferred to a horse-drawn wagon, which delivered the beer to customers. It cost $2.50 each trip for the teamster and his team of horses to deliver the beer to the boat or pick up the empties on the return trip. There was an additional seven-and-a-half cent charge for each pony keg loaded on or off the boat. In the winter, the beer was delivered by horse-drawn wagon over the ice, which eliminated a couple of steps and reduced the delivery expense.

From December 1883 to December 1884, according to Fitger's business journal, 4,572 pony kegs (561 barrels) were delivered to Superior at a total cost of $527, nearly one dollar a barrel. Sixty-three trips were made by boat and twenty trips were made over the ice.

The Fink Era Ends

Anneke's mother died in November 1884, and Fink sold his half of Lake Superior Brewery to Anneke for $18,000 in April 1885. Fink's life would never be the same. During his years at the brewery, Fink had served on the Duluth City Council as the Second Ward Alderman. He lost his re-election bid just one week after selling his shares. In July, he opened a saloon at 31 East Superior Street but stayed in the business for only a short time. In the early 1890s, he and a friend, Philip Graff, would open a brewery in Tower, Minnesota. Fink worked as the brewer for a few years, but the brewery was never successful, and he would end up leaving the brewing business entirely within a few years.

After leaving the brewery business, Fink's luck continued to wane. It was reported that he became involved in the timber business, but this cannot be verified. Fink did become involved in the mining business. A 1951 *Duluth News-Tribune* article about the "Point of Rocks," located at approximately 11th Avenue West and Michigan Street, stated, "The Point of Rocks has a silver lining. And it appears F. E. Kennedy, a pioneer Superior resident, found the Point of Rocks 'bonanza' in 1891. He wouldn't talk much about it, but claimed that the mine assayed at three hundred twelve dollars a ton. In 1893, the Duluth mining firm was incorporated. One of its major stockholders was Michael Fink, a man of many

Mathilde Anneke

Percy Anneke's mother was very talented and wrote novels, poetry, and drama. She used her knowledge and energy to fight for various social causes. While in Europe during the American Civil War, Mathilde wrote for publications sympathetic to the abolitionists. When she returned to America in 1865, she became a vocal spokesperson for women's rights, and through her efforts became nationally known among suffragettes. In 1904, legendary women's rights advocate Susan B. Anthony, speaking at the International Congress of Women's Rights in Berlin, stated, "It was through the influence of a German woman, Madam Mathilde Francisca Anneke, that I became a suffragette."

Mathilde founded the Madam Anneke's School, sometimes called the German French Academy, in Milwaukee. In later years, one of the girls who attended the school wrote about Mathilde, "All of us who had the joy of calling her our teacher had such great reverence for her that we considered her to have been the most important factor in our lives. It was not only what she taught but how she taught it. Her lessons were a source of boundless satisfaction. We went to them like to a festival."

After Mathilde's death in November 1884, Susan B. Anthony sent the Annekes a handwritten sympathy note. In the mid-1980s, the West German government recognized the accomplishments of Mathilde Francisca Anneke by issuing a special stamp in her honor.

Today, Fritz and Mathilde Anneke rest peacefully in Forest Home Cemetery in Milwaukee, only a stone's throw from the graves of August Fitger and his wife, Clara, and daughter Marion along with some Fitger in-laws, the Kirsts. Further down the same path in the cemetery rest the brewery moguls of Milwaukee—the names Best, Blatz, Pabst, Schlitz, and more are represented.

activities." Conrad Fink, Michael's son who worked at City Hall and still owned the Duluth Mining stock in 1951, told the reporter that his father was a mining advocate who once left Duluth to mine for gold in Halifax, Nova Scotia, but the mine never produced a cent's worth of ore.

After an extended bout of tuberculosis, Michael Fink died nearly a pauper in 1899 at his farm outside Duluth. His old friend and Brewery Saloon manager, Franz Heinrich, was with him when he died.

The New Partners

August Fitger and Percy Anneke were finally the owners of the Lake Superior Brewery, which they renamed "A. Fitger and Company Lake Superior Brewery." Anneke was thirty-five years old and Fitger was thirty-one. They both married in 1885, Anneke in January, Fitger in September. Anneke and his wife, Lydia, after living for a short time in Milwaukee, had moved to Duluth in May. The two couples moved in next door to each other in rented houses right across the street from the brewery.

Maintaining Wooden Kegs

In the spring of 1883, quarter barrels (eight-gallon kegs) were added to the pony kegs (four gallons) already used by the brewery. Even when empty, the kegs were very heavy compared to today's kegs because they were made of oak. The inside of each keg was pitched with resin so the beer never came in contact with the wood staves. Returned kegs were cleaned, piled in a pyramid, and continually sprinkled with water so the staves of the barrels would expand. These water-laden quarter barrels weighed nearly half as much as a quarter barrel full of beer, which weighed 170 pounds. Needless to say, pitching these barrels by hand into piles was a physically demanding job. (Below: The various barrels used at Fitger's required significant care and maintenance.)

CHAPTER 3

Bottles

Upon taking full control of the brewery from Michael Fink in the spring of 1885, Fitger and Anneke's first major project was the preparation and introduction of bottled beer, which they named "Export Beer." The first batch was brewed in early May, but the beer would be aged at least six months before bottling. Fitger's officially announced this new product in a newspaper ad on November 2, 1885.

Bottled beer opened up an entirely new market for Fitger's, because it allowed customers to purchase Fitger's Beer and bring it home, to picnics, or to parties. Before this time, beer would be purchased in pails from the local saloon and consumed immediately or it would go flat and become "skunky." A keg delivered to a home would have to be stored at the correct temperature or it also would become flat. Bottled beer, however, was pasteurized and had a shelf life of many weeks. Even with these distinct advantages, it would take bottled beer a long time to be accepted by the public. By 1890, five years after the introduction of bottled beer, bottling inventory including machinery, bottles, and corks would still be less than $1,000.

From the Kegs to the Bottles

The excise tax on beer was critical to the federal government, which had only three main sources of revenue at the time: the selling of bonds, the tariff, and the excise tax (there was no income tax for individuals or businesses

until 1912). The federal government collected the excise tax on beer by charging for issuance of stamps to be put

BOTTLED BEER.

A. FITGER & CO.
Lake Superior Brewery.

We take pleasure in announcing that we have fitted up a Bottling Department, and are prepared to fill orders for Export Beer. This Beer is brewed Especially for bottling purposes, of the Choisest Hops and Malt, and is at least six months old before before bottling, and is guaranteed by us to be pure and unadulterated. It is wholesome and palatable beverage, and can well be recommended to invalids. The Export Beer will be put up in cases of one or two dozen quarts, pints in cases of two dozen.

Orders are respectfully solicited and will receive prompt attention. Beer delivered to all parts of the city.
A. FITGER & CO.

A November 2, 1885, newspaper ad introducing bottled beer.

Bottle style dating to the late 1890s, after the invention of the crown or cap.

The Law of the Bottle

"Beer must not be bottled in a brewery or a warehouse or anywhere on the brewery or warehouse premises. This rule also prohibits washing or storing of bottles, steaming or all operations connected with bottling. Bottling must be done in a building completely distinct and separate from and having no communication with the brewery or warehouse. This means that the location and arrangement of the brewery or warehouse and the bottlery must be such that it is physically impossible to take the beer from the former to the latter without carrying the beer over the surface of a street or road which is a public highway and actually and commonly used by the public as a thoroughfare." These regulations would be replaced in 1892, when brewers could finally pump beer directly from the finishing cellars to the bottle house.

on kegs. The cost of the stamps was based on the volume of beer in the kegs. Therefore, extremely stringent mandates were designed to prevent businesses from cheating on these taxes by bottling beer directly from the vats without paying for keg stamps first. Fitger's had to make changes at the brewery to accommodate the new government requirements for bottling beer (see sidebar, above).

Fitger's constructed a new, temporary building for the bottling operation that was not in "communication" with the brewery. The first step of the bottling process required purchasing stamps for the kegs from the collector of revenue in the district located in Duluth, just as if the kegs were being prepared for sale to customers outside the brewery. The kegs were filled in the brewery building and the date perforated into the stamp, which was placed over the dispensing area. The stamped kegs had to be rolled out of the brewery to the other side of Superior Street, then rolled back and into the temporary bottle house. This fulfilled the requirement of "carrying the beer over…a public highway." The stamps could then be canceled, and the barrels were emptied directly into a large tank for bottling. The bottles were filled, a cork was inserted, the bottles were placed in hot water for thirty minutes for pasteurization, and then packaged in boxes for sale. As one can see, bottling was a very cumbersome process.

The actual bottles used were unique and required care when handled. Many of the quart and pint bottles were hand blown and had the name "Fitger" embossed on them. Fitger's also purchased wine bottles to use for beer bottles, because of their uniformity. Some of the earlier bottles even had their corks re-enforced with wire, much like champagne today. At first labels were not used, as they required additional expenses, such as labeling machines and a soaker to remove labels from returned empty bottles. Labels were added in the mid-1890s. Crowns or bottle caps were not invented until the late 1890s. Prior to that, the preferred stopper was a cork.

Apparently, a rumor went around that Fitger's used rubber stoppers; the brewery placed an ad in the newspaper to deny it, explaining that rubber would affect the beer's taste. In fact, brewers were hesitant to use anything new in the brewing process for fear of contaminating the beer. For

Fitger's "Export Beer" label, first used in 1885, would continue to be used into the 1900s, when "Natural Beer" replaced "Export Beer" as the mainstay product. When the brewery produced batches of specialized beer, they stamped "Bavarian" or "Pale Bohemian" in red ink over the "Export Beer" label.

example, before brewers would use new hoses to deliver the beer from the fermenting tanks to the aging tanks, the hoses were soaked in beer for at least thirty days. After the soaking, they would be used only in the initial stages of the brewing process. The oldest pumps in the brewery were always used in the finishing cellar for fear that a new pump might give out some type of odor that would affect the taste of the beer.

The new stock house, to the right of the brewery building originally built by Michael Fink.

New Stock House Changes Bottling Process

A two-and-a-half-story stock house measuring forty by seventy feet was built in 1886. The gable-roofed structure was designed by Chicago architect Fred Wolfe and faced with Lake Superior basalt, or bluestone, which would be used on all future brewery buildings along Superior Street. The stock house was located just to the southwest of the brewery, and the small yard left between the two buildings ensured it complied with federal regulations.

With the building of the new stock house, daily operations changed. In effect, the stock house became the brewery and the old brewery became the bottle house. The original brewery building continued to house the equipment for the first steps in the beer-making process—making the mash, adding water to the mash in the lauter tub, extracting the resulting liquid into the brew kettle, adding hops, and heating that mixture to produce the non-alcoholic base for beer, called wort. Since the wort was not beer, it could be transported directly to the stock house without crossing the street. In the stock house, yeast was added, which started the fermentation that made beer, and the beer was aged and filtered. Since there was no longer actual beer-making in the brewery building, bottling operations could be moved out of the temporary shed and into the brewery. As before, the kegs had to be rolled across the street from the stock house and back to the brewery building before bottling.

The bottling business was not only complicated, but also costly. Two dozen of the quart bottles in a wooden case weighed between fifty and sixty pounds, which increased shipping costs. Because of this and the cost of machinery and equipment, many breweries hired independent contractors to bottle the beer. Fitger's, however, bottled its own beer to ensure its quality.

A spring parade advertising the introduction of bock beer moves past the brewery and the new stock house.

CHAPTER 4

Buildings

The *Lake Superior News* reported on September 25, 1886, "A. Fitger and Company has plans prepared for their new beer warehouse and cooler.... They will shortly so increase the capacity of their brewery as to double its output."

Over the following years, increasing demand for Fitger's beer spurred the construction of several major buildings. Additional parcels of adjoining land were also purchased for future development.

In 1889, James Pierce built a thirty-two by ninety foot structure to serve as stables and a barn. The two-story frame building behind the brewery cost $1,500.

Ice Machine: Another Fitger's Innovation

Two buildings, the boiler house and the engine house (sometimes called the ice machine building), were constructed in 1890. Both were located behind the stock

The engine house. The boiler house is immediately behind it, next to the smokestack visible above the engine house.

The Fitger and Anneke Homes

In 1884, prior to his marriage, Fitger had purchased two lots on Seventh Avenue East and First Street from a John LaVaque. In February 1888, Fitger built a small home on his Seventh Avenue East property in which he and his wife, Clara, who was pregnant, lived with his wife's parents, Mr. and Mrs. Adam Kirst. The Kirsts would continue to live there after the Fitgers moved into their new home.

From 1892 to 1893, at a cost of $10,661.08, Fitger constructed a home for himself and Clara on the corner of Seventh Avenue East and First Street, which can still be seen today. Later he purchased an adjoining lot to the west of his property on First Street for additional yard space. He also purchased 175 feet of property across First Street from his home, to preserve his view of the brewery and Lake Superior, as well as several lots along the western side of Washington Avenue, which connected the corner of First Street and Seventh Avenue East with Superior Street at the eastern end of the brewery property. Eventually he built houses on the Washington Avenue property and rented them to employees.

The Fitger house facing First Street in 1897, before Fitger bought the lot next door for additional yard space. The smaller Seventh Avenue home he built first is visible on the right behind the larger house.

Fitger's home office in the First Street home, circa 1910, showing the fine craftsmanship of the furniture and the elaborate lighting fixtures. The large portraits above the bookcases are his parents, Peter (left) and Clara.

The Anneke family also moved into a new home, purchasing a house between Fifth and Sixth Avenues East on Second Street, in a neighborhood known as Ashtabula Heights at the time. The Fitgers and Annekes lived less than three blocks apart.

Anneke would later move to the Endion area of Duluth. When his son Marcel, who suffered from chronic tuberculosis, became a young teenager, Percy built him a beautiful summer home on Minnesota Point. Percy believed the fresh Lake Superior breezes would be beneficial for Marcel's health.

The Anneke house facing Second Street, summer 1897.

A casually furnished room in the Anneke house, adjoining the more formal dining room, August 1896.

The summer home built for Marcel Anneke's health. It still stands today near the Park Point recreation area entrance.

The interior of the Minnesota Point home provided a warm retreat.

house along the bluff above the railroad tracks. Trapphagen and Fitzpatrick were the architects for the boiler house. Mick Miller built the fifty-six by sixty foot structure at a cost of $7,000.

The ice machine was the first in Minnesota for a brewery, an innovation to ensure the quality of the beer. The ice machine didn't make blocks or cubes, but rather was a cooling system. It pumped cold water through pipes from the engine house to the stock house, where the beer was processed and stored. Ice harvesting continued on Lake Superior to supply customers with ice needed to transport or store their beer.

The engine house also contained a DC power plant that powered the ice machine, all other power equipment in the brewery, and served the Fitger and Anneke homes

The ice machine in 1891. The machine pumped cold water to the nearby stock house to keep the beer cool.

several blocks away before AC power was available throughout the city. Fitger's continued to use DC power to operate the elevators and cooling system even after AC power was available.

Brewery Expansion Continues

In 1892, Fitger's once again hired architects Trapphagen and Fitzpatrick, considered to be the best in Duluth. Over the next several years they would design three new buildings for the brewery. The first of these was a new brew house, which was attached to the southern corner of the original brewery building in 1892 and 1893. Because the brew house could not be "in communication" with the bottling operations in the old brewery building, there was no doorway between the two adjacent structures.

New buildings weren't the only projects at Fitger's. Major renovations were made to the older sections of the brewery. In fall 1894, the Brewery Saloon was enlarged and completely remodeled at the cost of $2,359.89. This remodeling made the saloon feel like a German "rathskeller" with ornate decorations and elaborate murals.

Two painters, Feodor von Leurzer and John Fery, spent numerous days painting the murals on the wall. Leurzer's uncle Karl, a very successful architect, an excellent amateur artist, and the closest friend of Feodor, was an interested observer during the painting of the murals. He later wrote von Leurzer's daughter Feodora, "Your father was commissioned to do a mural for the Dutch Room of the Fitger Brewery. This was a gorgeous old taproom with heavy oak tables, bottle glass windows and a big fireplace, stag antlers, heavy oak panels between planks, conviviality and warmth. I'm not sure if one or the other was the first commissioned to do the work but von Luerzer and the artist Fery each painted half around the upper walls of the room. It was a large room, so there was much space for both to demonstrate their skills.

"One end of the room is Fery who seizes the classical landscapes scenery, the formal beauty and design and the skillful, craftily cool orderliness that typifies much of his later work. The other end is von Leurzer and there the spirit changes. A world of fancy and fun and German legend give warmth and humor to the room. Much as I like Fery's work, when I go there I find myself enjoying and looking at von Leurzer's work the whole time. Little elves brew beer in huge copper kettles and climb vast kegs. Elderly, slightly inebriated monks leer over their drinking mugs. Cherubs and mincing barmaids cavort joyously."

In 1896, the focus returned to new buildings and the work of Trapphagen and Fitzpatrick. A settling room, forty by twenty-five feet, was built behind the stock house.

Strategies for Increasing Beer Sales

Fitger's Beer had a reputation as being an excellent beer. The brewery used only natural ingredients and a process

that did not boil the beer, which made the beer taste better. Quality production increased Fitger's market share.

Other factors also contributed to increase sales. In the 1890s, the Iron Range, consisting of the Mesabi, Vermilion and, later, the Cuyuna Range, was growing rapidly. Cities were developed and with cities came saloons. One of the best strategies to increase sales was to establish "tied houses," a system still used in Europe. A saloon was tied to a brewery, only serving that brewery's beer.

Location was important for a tied house to be successful. Fitger's believed corners were ideal because this allowed the saloon to have an entrance on the street and also one on the avenue. The entrance on the avenue was mainly for people who would come in during the evening to get a pail of beer, called a growler. People living in the immediate area, many of them immigrants, liked beer with their supper and would send junior down to the

The renovated Brewery Saloon in 1907. The Dutch Room is visible through the archway at the back.

The DC power plant. Engineers were responsible for the plant, the brewery machinery, and blowing the steam whistles signalling starting, lunch, and quitting times.

local pub to pick up a pail of beer. The pails would often be greased, reducing the foam so more beer would fit in the pail.

When a brewery found a good location, it would buy or lease the land or building. The brewery would then find a respectable individual to manage the saloon and furnish the bar, the back bar, and all of the necessary equipment. The proprietor's main job was to dispense the beer. The proprietor would pay rent to the brewery and sign a legal document stating that all he owned was his hat on the hat rack. One interesting marketing gimmick used was the free lunch—bar owners offered a free lunch with a nickel glass of beer. This was available at the tied houses and also the independent saloons. All the breweries in Duluth used these strategies to sell beer.

Karl Leurzer and Brautigan Gardens

Leurzer moved to Duluth in 1889, canoeing with his painting equipment and a friend all the way from Cleveland, Ohio. He married the daughter of Adolph Brautigan, owner of Duluth's first amusement park, Brautigan Gardens. The Fitger and Anneke families frequented the park, which was located on the shore of Lake Superior between London Road and the lake, extending from 29th Avenue East to 31st Avenue East. It was a popular destination for most of the city's organizations, including lodges, fraternal societies, and churches. Many families rode in buggies, walked, or pushed baby carriages two-and-a-half miles from town to visit the Gardens. Brautigan Gardens boasted an open-air dancing pavilion, an outdoor bowling lane, a variety of equipment for gymnasts, a shooting gallery, an outdoor theater, a German-style beer garden, and many other activities, including an outdoor curling facility for the winter months.

Leurzer built the outdoor theater at Brautigan Gardens and painted beautiful murals inside several homes on the property. He later traveled out West to do a commissioned painting of redwood trees owned by the Whiteside family of Duluth and fell in love with Coeur d'Alene, Idaho. Brautigan was killed when he tried to shoot a hawk but tripped and shot himself on October 28, 1895. Shortly thereafter, the Gardens closed permanently, and Leurzer and his wife moved to Idaho.

The outdoor bowling lane at Brautigan Garden (roughly 31st Avenue East and London Road), one of many activities available at Duluth's first amusement park.

CHAPTER 5

Duluth's Breweries

In 1896, Reiner Hoch built and opened Duluth Brewing and Malting Company in the West End of Duluth (now called Lincoln Park). Hoch and a partner, Charles Meeske, had brewing experience before moving to Duluth, including a business in Milwaukee and, after that, the Upper Peninsula Brewing Company, which had very successful breweries in Marquette and Negaunee, Michigan. Meeske would re-join Hoch at Duluth Brewing and Malting in 1916, after early prohibition in the Upper Peninsula forced him to close the breweries there.

Outside Interests

From the beginning of their partnership, Fitger and Anneke worked long and hard hours at the brewery to make sure their investment proved successful. But even as the brewery continued to thrive and grow, they also had other interests and made time for those pursuits as well.

Travel was important for both families, whether for business or recreation. Fitger was very involved in the United States Brewers Association, which required many trips throughout the United States to attend meetings. From time to time he would take his wife and family along on meetings in New Orleans, New York, or elsewhere. Both families made trips to Europe on various occasions. Fitger would often visit his family in Bremen and from there travel to other parts of Europe, notably Berlin, Switzerland, and Italy. Anneke enjoyed the Mediterranean area and would often vacation with his family there. Both visited Central America and checked out potential mining sites in the area as their business interests diversified.

The Fitgers and Annekes also enjoyed music—both frequented the Duluth Opera House—and would invite musicians and guests to their homes for an evening of enlightening entertainment. They often attended lectures, which were popular at the time. After giving a lecture in Duluth, Susan B. Anthony once wrote a letter to Anneke's sister, Hertha, noting how pleasant it had been to see Percy and his wife there.

The Turnverien Society, or the Turner Society, was another interest of both Fitger and Anneke. The Turner Society, a German Society organization, emphasized physical and mental health. The original Turner Hall burned down in the fire that had destroyed Duluth's first grain elevator, Elevator "A," on November 27, 1896. The fire had also threatened the brewery. A new hall was constructed in Ashtabula Heights on Sixth Avenue East and Third Street. The Society featured singing, drama, acting, dance, and athletic groups. During the year, the Duluth Turner Society would compete in singing, dancing, and gymnastics against the Turner Societies from New Ulm, St. Paul, Minneapolis, and other German communities in Minnesota.

A Northern Steamship Company wine list from the late 1890s shows Fitger's central inspiration; his red star follows the same lines as the steamship's logo, which is also centered on a ship.

August Fitger's sketch for a new Fitger's Export Beer label.

The Duluth Brewing and Malting Company had a substantial amount of working capital to support its business. Because of this, August Fitger was concerned that a "beer war" could begin between the various breweries in the area. To stave off any price war or raiding of one another's customers, Fitger established an association of the breweries.

The association met every Saturday morning to discuss business and review donation requests. Members decided how much money or beer should be donated for various clubs and community events. Whenever there was a natural disaster, such as a forest fire, the organization would donate to the cause. The association achieved its goals—communication between all the breweries allowed everyone a chance for success, and the donations created a good public image for the breweries.

Fitger was becoming the public spokesman for the beer industry in Duluth. When the state legislature significantly increased the license fees for brewers and retail saloons to $1,000 a year in cities of the first class, which now included the City of Duluth, Fitger and Anneke publicly expressed their displeasure. In doing so, they gained a lot of friends and customers among the public saloon owners, who formerly had done little or no business with them. The license fee, although an unwanted expense, was thus a mixed blessing for the company.

Fitger Redesigns the Beer Label

In 1897, Fitger redesigned the label for Fitger's Export Beer. He was aboard a steamship when he conceived the idea; he drew the new label on the front of a menu of the Northern Steamship Company owned by James J. Hill.

He cut out the picture of the S.S. *Duluth* from an existing label, along with the words Export, Beer, Guaranteed, and Perfect, and pasted them all onto the menu. He added the five-point red star in ink, and drew the border and decorative scrolls with a blue pencil. Before adding the letters in black ink at the bottom, he penciled in some guidelines.

Fitger didn't use this new design until after 1910; at that time he would also drop the hops and barley sprigs that had adorned Fitger's labels since 1885.

Duluth and Fitger's Boom in the 1890s

The 1890s were very good for Fitger and Anneke. In 1890, the brewery was appraised at $77,183.55. The land occupied by the brewery was valued at $30,300.90. Fitger's Brewery owned real estate in Tower valued at $300. By the end of the decade, the brewery's appraisal had increased to $250,680.44, and the brewery real estate was valued at $68,120. A. Fitger and Company also owned twenty-three additional parcels of land in and out of the city of Duluth. In the first fifteen years of the Fitger and Anneke partnership, they had expanded from one building to eight buildings along Superior Street and the lake.

The newest of those was the last of the three Trapphagen–Fitzpatrick buildings. In 1899, stock house #2 was built to the southwest and adjacent to what then became known as stock house #1. The large $10,000 structure measured fifty feet wide by ninety-five feet deep and stood two stories high on the street side and three stories high on the lakeside. It was another sign of Fitger's continued growth.

The brewery's output had gone from 5,205 barrels during the first full year of operation in 1883 to approximately 30,000 barrels in 1900, an increase of nearly six hundred percent. Fitger and Anneke were shrewd businessmen and had turned a risky adventure into a very successful and well-diversified business.

During the same period, Duluth's population grew to fifty thousand inhabitants. The city limits now stretched from Lakeside in the east all the way out to Gary-New Duluth in the west, almost thirty miles long. There were forty-one churches in the city of Duluth, thirty-four schools (public and private), and more than one hundred saloons. Business continued to expand during the decade. Iron ore was discovered on the Mesabi Range, and a railroad was built to bring ore into the newly constructed Duluth docks. Lumbering also became a big business.

Brewery Nearly Sold to British Interests

During the 1880s and 1890s, British investors purchased millions of dollars worth of breweries throughout the

The Northern Steamship Company's extensive wine and drink menu included Fitger's Pale Bohemian.

Fitger's Farm

Fitger started building a farm complex in 1899 and first referred to it as "Section 16," which had originally been earmarked for a township school. A newspaper article stated, "Fitger's farm is ten miles north of the Lester River Valley Road. There are 15 acres under cultivation with an additional ten acres cleared around the summer cottage as a preventative against forest fires." This was good foresight on the part of Fitger; the cleared area protected the farm from damage during the Cloquet–Moose Lake Fire that destroyed other parts of Lakewood (see Chapter 10 sidebar, "The Cloquet–Moose Lake Fire of 1918").

The Fitgers enjoyed the Lester River area. Fitger had often sent his wife and children to the Lester Park Hotel in the summer for a vacation of four to five weeks. The Hotel was located at what now is Sixty-first Avenue East and London Road, just west of the Lester River. Today it is an easy drive; in those days, however, a heavily forested area separated the brewery from the Lester River. The preferred choice of transportation was boat, or the more adventurous could take the so-called road between Fitger's and the Lester River.

Elmhurst, the Fitger farm on the Lester River.

The Lester River Hotel.

Fitger eventually named his acreage in Lakewood "Elmhurst," which reminded him of his boyhood youth in Delmenhorst, Germany. He visited the farm as often as he could. In the early days, he would ride on horseback there and back the same day or sometimes stay overnight. In winter, he would take the horse and sleigh.

When he purchased his first automobile, a Phantom, he had his chauffeur drive him to Elmhurst. Fitger never drove himself. He also built a beautiful summer home on the property along Lester River featuring Germanic interior decor.

He sold his farm in 1928 to George Barnum, whose family had roots in Duluth dating back to the 1860s and had made its fortune in the grain trade. The town of Barnum, south of Duluth, was named in his honor. Interestingly, a family descendant, also named George Barnum, would be an early partner of John Ferris when Ferris invested in Fitger's Brewery in 1969.

The crew takes a break from building a log cabin at Elmhurst. The supervisor in the suit is John Beerhalter, Fitger's master brewer from 1902 to 1944.

The inside of the Elmhurst summer home was designed for comfortable entertaining.

United States. In August of 1899, A. Fitger and Company received a letter from two attorneys in St. Louis, Missouri, asking if Fitger's was interested in selling the business for cash to a private concern. The letter further stated, "We also ask you to give us in writing the condition of your trade, location of plant and general information. This writer will make arrangements, if such be satisfactory to yourself, to call on you in person at an early date. For our mutual benefit, we suggest that this matter be treated strictly confidential."

In October 1899, an agreement was drafted between Fitger, Anneke, and the legal representatives of the group that sought to purchase the brewery. There were many provisions in this draft, and the stated purchase price was $285,000. One provision stated, "Upon request of the party of the second part [the people buying the brewery] August Fitger and Percy Anneke will enter into appropriate contracts to serve and work for the new corporation for a term not to exceed five years and with salaries to be agreed upon with the new corporation." The last provision stated, "This option shall be void unless accepted and acted upon before January first, 1900." Fitger and Anneke, who were still principal owners of Fitger's Brewery, did not sign the purchase agreement. They felt that the cooperation they had fostered among the Duluth breweries and the strong regional economy promised greater financial rewards if they kept the brewery. This was fortunate for Fitger's and its legacy, because most of the British-owned breweries in America eventually went bankrupt.

Percy Anneke (standing) and August Fitger in 1903.

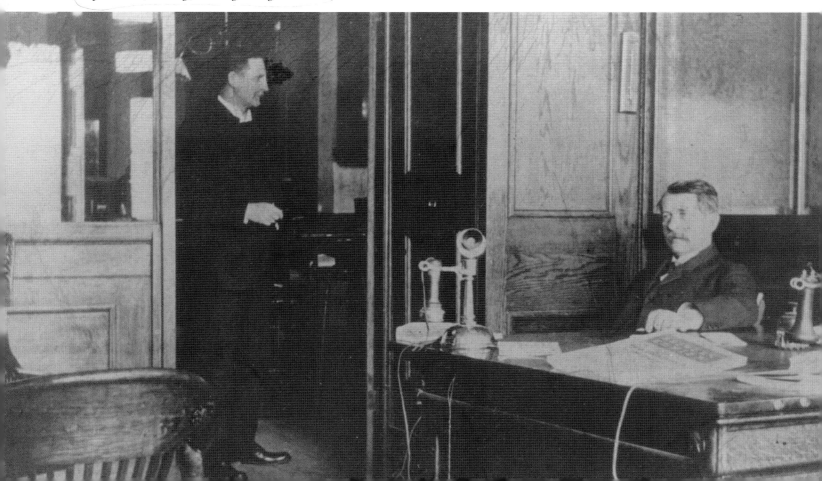

PART II

The Dawn of a New Century

Fitger's official letterhead in the early 1900s. The ice and engine houses were actually much further west, behind the stock houses. The stables depicted at left were never built. Note the Aerial Transfer Bridge and Duluth Ship Canal in the background.

CHAPTER 6

Master Brewer

During the first decade of the new century, Fitger's barrelage would increase more than 250 percent to reach 78,000 barrels by 1910. With this also came more competition. Two new breweries, one in Virginia and the People's Brewery in West Duluth, were built by 1910. At this time, there were two breweries on the Range, three in Duluth, two in Superior, and one in Ashland, Wisconsin.

Fitger's employees pose proudly in front of the new mill house. Just visible on the left is the original Brewery Saloon.

Eventually, the brewery in Tower closed and the Klinkert Brewery in Superior was torn down because the owners sold the real estate to a railroad. Duluth Brewing and Malting bought the Klinkert saloon business, fixtures, horses, and wagons for approximately $25,000 and used them for their own expanded trade in Superior. The final surge of building at Fitger's also occurred in the first decade of the twentieth century.

The New Mill House

Because of the growing demand for beer and an increase in competition, Fitger's continued to expand. A new mill house was built in 1900 to accommodate this expansion.

The new mill house connected the Brewery Saloon, part of the original 1881 Fink Brewery, on the east with stock house #1 on the west. It was twenty-five feet wide,

ninety-five feet deep and four stories high on the Superior Street side plus the basement on the lower level. At the same time the mill house was constructed, workers also remodeled the brew house—built from 1892 to 1893—which stood immediately behind the new building. The combined project cost $22,844.

Fitger Hires Beerhalter as Master Brewer

In 1902, Fitger made a key addition to brewery personnel. A tall, husky twenty-eight-year-old German arrived to assume the position of master brewer. If his size didn't impress Fitger, his name did—John Beerhalter. What better name for a brewmaster?

Beerhalter had spent ten years working at various breweries in St. Louis and his native Germany, beginning in Augsburg, Germany, in 1889, before enrolling at the prestigious Wahl-Henius Institute of Fermentology in

The Beerhalter Family

John Blaise Beerhalter, like Fitger, had emigrated from Germany as a young man. He was very bright; at age 11, in 1885, he finished the local school in Kottspiel, Wuerttemberg, Germany. But unlike Fitger and Anneke, he was from a farming family, which did not provide the means for a college education or the cultural and artistic influences the Fitger and Anneke families enjoyed.

Beerhalter's father, Moritz, had died when John was four years old. His mother, Mary Ann Hummel, and his six older sisters ran the forty-acre farm until his oldest sister, Katherine, married Franz Klotzbuecher from the neighboring village and he took over. Because Klotzbuecher also was a cooper, Beerhalter was able to finish his apprenticeship in making beer barrels at home. A cooper makes barrels by soaking wood, forming the staves by hand, and applying metal bands to hold the shape. After completing the apprenticeship, Beerhalter did not take a job as a cooper, however. He moved to Hall, Germany, for a two-year brewing course.

During the apprenticeship, he worked at the brewery for room and board and seventy-five cents a week. After finishing his brewing apprenticeship, Beerhalter worked at two breweries in Germany before leaving for St. Louis in September 1892 to join three of his married sisters who had emigrated earlier. Before the end of the year, he married Amelia Schwab. During the next seven years, he worked at numerous breweries in the St. Louis area. He was low in seniority and moved from brewery to brewery in search for a better position while working construction between brewery jobs. He and his wife had three children before she and a baby died during childbirth in 1900.

Beerhalter would marry again in 1909 to Martha Callies of Cleveland. They had three children. The two sons would have long careers at Fitger's.

Outdoor Recreation

Beerhalter accepted the job at Fitger's not only because it was a great opportunity, but also because he loved to hunt and fish. Northern Minnesota provided some of the best hunting and fishing in the United States, and Beerhalter's new bosses were both avid outdoorsmen. Every fall Fitger and Anneke would hunt and fish in the Schultz Lake area, along with a number of other outdoor enthusiasts. They would follow the old Vermilion Trail for some twenty miles and detour slightly west a few miles to where they and their friends had built a log hunting cabin.

Fitger and Anneke's log hunting cabin near Schultz Lake, October 1897. Fitger is seated at right, holding the dog's collar.

Anneke at the hunting cabin, second from left, standing and holding a pipe, October 1897.

A successful outing for Anneke, with pipe, and his fishing partner.

Chicago in 1901. Fitger would later say this was a better institution than Weihenstephan in Germany, probably because it included modern techniques for brewing. The brewing techniques Beerhalter had learned in Germany were primitive compared to the techniques used in facilities like Fitger's. Beerhalter noted in his remembrances,

"I was then ten years in the United States and never had a college education." But he received the highest grades in history at Wahl-Henius, which taught some students in German and some in English. The English class included five brewery owners' sons who all graduated either from Yale or Harvard.

Beer Time, Beerhalter, and Boards

Beer time was an age-old custom at breweries, dating back centuries. It was ten to fifteen minutes in the morning and in the afternoon for employees to sit down and have a beer. Of course, many employees would have coffee or whatever they brought in their lunch buckets, but it was still known as "beer time." Brewers discontinued this practice by the late 1960s. Coopen Johnson recalls the old days:

"Mr. Beerhalter demanded and received respect from all employees at the brewery. When I first started at the brewery in 1948, an old time carpenter, Carl Leland, told me, 'Always carry something when walking in the yard.' The yard was an area behind the office and bottling department where trucks and railroad cars were loaded. If Mr. Beerhalter would see someone just walking in the yard, he would call the employee to the office and ask what his purpose was. Carl always carried a board.

"I'm sure he carried the same board for many years. And I realized sometime later that Carl would go from the carpenter shop to the beer hole [the break room] and then to the bottle house for beer time. Now beer time was staggered at the brewery. The brew house and the wash house employees had their beer break earlier than the bottle house. So Carl Leland had two beer breaks in the morning and two in the afternoon. And in the yard he carried that board the whole time I was at the brewery and I'm sure many years before."

Carl Leland, holding his famous board, and the rest of the crew in the yard.

The position of master brewer was especially important at this time; the previous four brewmasters or superintendents had been terminated for being too bossy, conceited, lazy, or impish. Beerhalter proved to be a very capable employee and Fitger trusted him highly. Beerhalter's knowledge and skills in brewing became renowned. He had a knack for finding problems in the brewing process and remedying them. Over the ensuing years, many Minnesota brewers asked Fitger if Beerhalter could assist them in finding solutions to their brewing problems.

In his memoirs, Beerhalter recalled his first days at Fitger's. "I was put in full charge of production, including delivery. We had at the time from 18 to 24 horses. I managed the whole brewery with the exception of the office. I also brewed all beer in the first five years.... All beer was made during the cold winter months as we had no way of cooling the hot beer in the summer. Our working time was from 2:00 A.M. to 6:00 P.M. When making malt, which was also done during the winter, I had to turn the kiln on at 10:00 P.M. This took about thirty minutes. In my second year, I was in charge of brewing and

The low structure on the left is the 1881 brewery, home of the Brewery Saloon. The tallest structure in the middle is the mill house, built in 1900. To the immediate right of the mill house is stock house #1, which, after the 1902 remodel, no longer had a gable roof.

malting. We had no steam or mashing machinery. All mashing was done by hand with paddles and the iron kettle was fired by wood or coal. When the brew was finished, I had to carry the spent grains to the cow barn about one block up the hill in the snow."

In Beerhalter, Fitger finally found a brewmaster he could count on. Along with P.C. Schmidt as the brewery lawyer, Ben Grimm as sales manager, and Walter Johnson as the brewery auditor, Fitger now had a dedicated staff that allowed him to leave the brewery at any time and know the company was always in good hands. In particular, Fitger relied on Grimm.

Fitger's Continues Steady Expansion

Building projects at the brewery were virtually non-stop during the first decade of the twentieth century. Six new buildings more than doubled the size of the brewery. In addition, there was extensive remodeling of the existing buildings.

Beerhalter's first construction responsibilities began immediately in 1902 with major remodeling of the stock houses. The result would bring a new cohesiveness to the style of the Superior Street buildings and significantly expand the space for brewing operations.

The original gable roof of the two-and-a-half-story stock house #1 was torn off. A full third floor with a flat

The remodeled stock houses #1 and #2, with the four-story mill house on the left. The varying colorations on the new facade indicate their original rooflines. Eventually, weathering erased the color differences. The houses on the right were later removed for further expansion.

roof replaced the old attic area under the gable. The two-story stock house #2 also had a third floor added. Decorative trim and matching stone now tied these structures together and dwarfed the original cream-colored brick brewery and saloon.

Fitger's hired nationally renowned brewery architect Louis Lehle of Chicago in 1903 to design the new wash house and racking room. They were located next to the boiler house and engine house (the ice machine building). The large two-story building was built with brick, rather than the Lake Superior basalt exterior of the newer buildings along Superior Street. At 118 feet long, the wash house and racking room equaled the length of the mill house and stock houses combined. At the time it was built, the new building could be seen from Superior Street because there were no buildings between it and the street. Fitger's would continue to use Lehle to design the rest of its major building projects in the following years.

The Copper Kettle

The brewing kettle was always the showpiece of a brewery. In 1903, Fitger had a beautiful new hand-tooled brew kettle made in Chicago. It was installed during another major remodeling of the mill house and brew house, as growing sales required adjustments for increasing capacity in all segments of the brewery operations.

The new kettle had a capacity of 240 barrels, which was considered a large kettle in those days. The M. Fink

The interior of the wash house, where kegs were cleaned.

& Company–Lake Superior Brewery had started in 1882 with a kettle that held only about 30 barrels. (The largest brew kettle in Minnesota was at Duluth Brewing and Malting Company, with a capacity of nearly 500 barrels; that kettle was sold for scrap when the brewery was demolished in the early 1980s to make room for Interstate 35.) Every two weeks, two employees would take four hours to polish the new kettle to a high sheen.

Fitger's shiny new brewing kettle in 1901. From left to right, John Beerhalter Sr., an unidentified man, and Joe Polski, a superintendent at the brewery. Also visible is the lauter tub, where water was added to the mash before the liquid entered the kettle.

CHAPTER 7

Incorporation

The A. Fitger and Company Lake Superior Brewery became a corporation in 1904 and was renamed The Fitger Brewing Company. The corporation replaced the formal partnership Fitger and Anneke had signed in 1892. The first stock certificate was issued on January 1, 1904, to Fitger, for 2,495 shares worth $100 each.

The second certificate was issued to Anneke for the same number of shares. State law required at least three shareholders to set up a corporation, so a third certificate, for ten shares, was sold to Ben Grimm, sales manager since 1887. Fitger and Anneke would eventually purchase the shares back from the Grimm in 1917 and

Fitger Brewing Company Stock Certificate No. 1.

Left: The covered loading dock behind the wash house and racking room, circa 1920.

Bottom: The Fitger's railroad spur had two tracks running between the brewery's buildings. The railroad car is parked beside the boiler house.

Fitger and Anneke Diversify

The robust economy of the times provided opportunities for Fitger and Anneke to invest in other businesses both for financial gain and also as a hedge against the growing threat of the temperance movement. They had to be very selective with their investments because this was also an era filled with many "get rich quick" schemes. Fitger and Anneke participated in many investments with varying results.

One of these investments was Northern Light Mining and Development Company, located right outside Port Arthur, Canada, which was a Lake Superior port about forty miles east of the Minnesota border. The company was owned and operated by a group of Duluthians headed by John Gonska, a dear friend of both Fitger and Anneke. This particular gold field never produced enough gold to make a profit, but they did, however, acquire 567 acres of property.

Other investments included Balkan Rubber Company, Velda Drug Company, Northwest Jobbers Credit Bureau, United States and Dominion Life Insurance Company, Hotel Androy in Superior, Hotel Duluth, T and B Mining and Smelting Company in Arizona, and other real estate.

Fitger and Anneke, along with eight other businessmen, also partnered in the Buhl Investment Company by purchasing the first and second additions in the city of Buhl. The plan was to subdivide the property and sell the parcels of land. This proved to be successful, and from 1905 to 1920 dividends were received on a semi-annual basis.

There was one notable investment Fitger did not make. In his diary on September 12, 1906, Fitger wrote, "Dwan asked me to go into some speculation with him." The company that John Dwan had cofounded in 1902 was having financial trouble and Dwan was looking for investors. Fitger went on to note his decision: "Nit," meaning no. The "speculation" that Fitger did not invest in was Minnesota Mining & Manufacturing Company (3M). Today, 3M is one of the most successful companies in the United States.

give five shares each to their sons, Arnold Fitger and Victor Anneke.

Railroad Spur Comes to Fitger's Yard

Extension of a railroad spur into the brewery simplified the distribution process of Fitger's Beer. Arnold, Fitger's son, drove in the last spike on the spur. On September 25, 1904, Fitger noted in his diary: "The first engine in our yard."

The railroad spur saved the brewery tens of thousands of dollars in labor costs alone each year. In the summer, it was common for the brewery to load sixty to seventy railroad cars a month. The spur helped quality control because the cold beer from the cellars could be loaded directly into insulated cars, not allowing the beer to warm and possibly become damaged. Previously, all the beer sold outside the immediate area was loaded by Fitger's employees onto horse-drawn wagons, driven to the railroad yards, and off-loaded to the railroad cars for shipment. Similarly, a horse-drawn wagon had been sent down to the railroad yard to collect all the empties, beer-making supplies, and brewing equipment and bring them back to the brewery to be unloaded.

The Fitger's spur became the most popular run for railroad crews; on a hot summer day the crews had a chance for a cold brew in the beer hole, the employees' break room. Prior to Fitger's, the railroad crew would stop at one of the many meat wholesalers on Michigan Street to pick up a couple rings of baloney. Once they arrived at Fitger's, the crew would go to the beer hole and cook the baloney in a tub of hot water that employees primarily used to warm up their tankards during beer time. Beer and sausage was a bartered lunch enjoyed by both the railroad crew and the Fitger's employees. This custom continued into the 1950s when Fitger's dispensed with beer time. During the Christmas season, Fitger would reward the railroad crew with locally made El Coro cigars. He felt the railroad men were an important part of the Fitger family, even though they were not actual employees.

New Smokestack

In 1905, Fitger's built a towering new smokestack (photo page 135). The construction required rebuilding a portion of the boiler house for a total cost of $6,000. The original boiler house had been built for $7,000 in 1890.

Building the large smokestack was a complex project. The foundation went down sixteen feet to bedrock along the Lake Superior bluff. The smokestack itself rose more than one hundred feet above the ground, the tallest stack in Duluth. The height of the smokestack at any brewery was a matter of pride. Fitger and Anneke, as usual, wanted only the best for Fitger's, so they hired a specialist, architect George E. Thompson of Minneapolis, to design the imposing structure.

Fitger's branch in East Grand Forks, Minnesota, in 1906.

New Ice House

Fitger's installation of the first ice machine in Minnesota in 1891 had ended the need for harvested ice for brewery operations. The ice Fitger's still harvested from Lake Superior to sell to their customers was stored in an ice-house, but that space was now needed to expand brewing capacity.

In 1906, a new three-story wooden ice house was constructed to store the harvested ice. The ice house was built at the western edge of Fitger's Brewery property across a work yard from the west end of stock house #2. Eventually, the beer business became so competitive that Fitger's gave the ice to its customers for free as an incentive to keep their business.

New Bottle House:
Fitger's Largest Single Project

In 1907, the building boom at Fitger's continued with construction of the new bottle house (which is the major portion of today's Fitger's Inn) about 35 feet eastward of

The new ice house on the left, stock house #2 on the right.

Top: The new bottle house under construction, revealing the massive steel girders and huge blocks of bluestone.

Bottom: The completed bottle house, August 14, 1922; the office building, which was tucked into the space between the new bottle house and the 1881 brewery, is attached to the right of the bottle house.

the 1881 brewery building on Superior Street. The bottle house was 118 feet long, 75 feet deep, and 3 stories high, matching the combined size of the mill house/brew house and stock houses #1 and #2. Fitger's Brewery now stretched approximately 340 feet along Superior Street.

The exterior of the bottle house was the same Lake Superior basalt used on all of the Superior Street buildings that Fitger and Anneke constructed; the older brewery building of cream-colored brick was now surrounded by bluestone. Fitger believed using local material and labor was important from a business standpoint because most

of these businesses and employees were also potential Fitger's customers.

In 1890, Congress had eliminated the burdensome regulation of rolling beer kegs across a public thoroughfare before moving beer into the bottling area, allowing breweries to use a pipeline to connect the brewing operation with the bottling facility. Accordingly, a new pipeline was installed at Fitger's to pump beer from the finishing cellar on the basement level of stock house #2 into what was called a "government cellar" in the lower west end of the bottle house.

The new laws were still not that easy for the brewers, however. The government cellar (located at the foot of the

The bottle house, December 1, 1909. The crew poses by the conveyor belt that brought filled beer cases to the lower area for shipment or storage. The cases were made of wood.

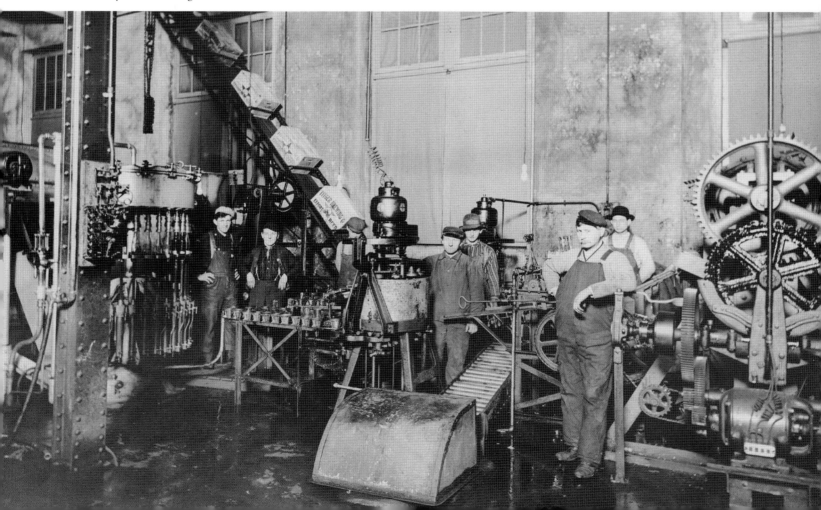

stairs from today's Fitger's Inn lobby to the courtyard level) was locked by the government collector, who was the only person with a key. Behind the locked door were two large tanks with cylindrical gauges. Prior to bottling beer, Fitger's had to contact the tax collector, who would come to the brewery, unlock the door, and, after he was told how much beer was to be bottled, collect the proper amount of tax. This system was later eliminated when meters were installed. But then government agents conducted surprise inspections to make sure all the beer went through the meters. As late as the 1960s, federal agents would dress in old clothes and crawl through the space around the

pipeline to make sure there weren't any areas where beer could be dispensed without passing through the meter.

The New Fitger's Office Building

Fitger and Anneke needed a larger office to accommodate the growing brewery business as well as the management of their other ventures. Louis Lehle, who had designed the wash house and racking room in 1903, was hired to build something extraordinary. The new office building was constructed in 1908, filling in the thirty-five foot gap between the 1881 brewery building and the bottle house. It matched the three-story height of the adjacent bottle

The office building's elaborate grillwork enclosure. L. M. Hansen, who served over forty years as Fitger's office manager, is at the window in the center. (Note the cuspidor, or spittoon, at the lower right.)

house and was made of brownstone and bluestone to blend with the existing buildings.

The center of the two-story main lobby was the cashier area, which was surrounded by detailed grillwork similar to bank cages of the era. The office staff handled all of the brewery's business as well as the numerous investment interests and real estate properties owned by Fitger and Anneke. Fitger's also provided loans to employees from the office, and customers would drop off rent or loan payments there. Even customers could apply for loans.

A two-tiered vault featured a hand-painted Fitger's seal on the security door and required a ladder to reach the second tier. In those days, the size of the vault was considered a sign of one's business success. Fitger had the vault built larger than the vaults in the other two Duluth breweries.

Behind the cashier area and vault on the main level was the boardroom overlooking Lake Superior with a fireplace inside and a balcony outside. The boardroom featured a custom-made oak table and an enormous painting by Arthur Fitger, August Fitger's brother who lived in Bremen, Germany. Every Monday morning, August and Percy would meet in the boardroom, check their pocket watches to make sure they were "in time" with one another, and weigh themselves. Finally, the plan of the week would then be decided.

The top level of the office building provided a lunch area for employees, a small library with comfortable chairs, and a recreation area with exercise equipment for individual or group workouts. There was also a meeting room for sales personnel. These areas were sometimes used for after-work activities, including dances.

In those days, most office workers were men. Smoking wasn't in vogue, but chewing tobacco was. Cuspidors were placed throughout the office for employ-

ees and visitors. The most important people had huge brass cuspidors with wide rims. The not-so-important individuals had smaller brass cuspidors. And the least-influential employees only had porcelain cuspidors.

Today, the main floor of the office building is the lobby of Fitger's Inn. The vault and a portion of the original grillwork, as well as the two-story columns and massive skylight, can still be seen there. The boardroom is available for meetings or private parties.

Right: The two-tiered vault as it appears today, still in use as a checkroom and for storing hotel equipment and supplies.

The Fitger Artists

Arthur Fitger was an internationally known historical painter and writer (Emil was also well respected for his writing). Many of Arthur's paintings still remain in the Fitger family. His last painting, the large masterpiece of Bacchus, Roman god of wine, hung over the mantle in the Fitger's boardroom until it disappeared during the redevelopment of the brewery in 1983; its location remains unknown. A large sketch now hangs in its place (see page iv).

Arthur's large sketch of Gambrenius (left), Flemish "King of Beers," (on display today in the lobby of Fitger's Inn), was to be a model for a statue that August planned for an elaborate rooftop garden at Fitger's. The garden was never built but Fitger's letterhead from the early part of the twentieth century (see page 30) depicts the sculpture and cupola atop the center portion of the brewery.

Gambrenius, Flemish "King of Beers," as sketched by Arthur Fitger to act as a model for a statue that was never built. (A photo of a sketch by Fitger appears on page iv, opposite the contents page.)

CHAPTER 8

Diversification

It was a gala event indeed when the Fitger Brewing Company held the grand opening of the Hotel Fitger in Bovey, Minnesota, in 1908 (incidentally, Bovey was named for the Minneapolis lumberman who platted the town). The hotel was considered the best in Itasca County and one of the best on the Iron Range.

The Fitger Company employed a Mr. Grimpo as the hotel's manager, and the two-story building had forty-five rooms, a dining hall, and, of course, a bar. For the grand opening, residents were invited to attend a dinner and dance at a dollar a plate. The hotel was initially successful, but in the later years it encountered some major obstacles. One of the main problems was the city's sewage system. Bovey had a cesspool for sewage treatment that never worked well and because of the continual problems the hotel would be forced to close after fifteen years of operation.

Other than the Hotel Fitger in Bovey and the Spalding Hotel in Crosby, Fitger's owned many hotels which were smaller in size and named after the town or a manager who had a small interest in the business, such as the O'Neill Hotel in Chisholm and the Ollila Hotel in Nashwauk. Single men who worked in the mines occupied these hotels and would spend their recreation time in the hotel saloons. When a town would spring up on the Range, the new communities would often ask Fitger's Brewery or Duluth Brewing and Malting to build a hotel

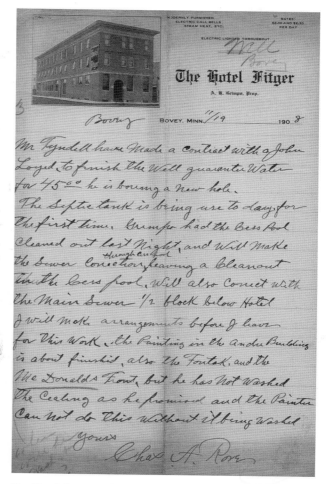

The Hotel Fitger stationery. The note details some of the work being done on the hotel's new septic system, which never worked properly.

The Fitger and Anneke Children

Top: Victor Anneke (left) and two of his children, Jean and Carlo, pose with Count von Luckner, a World War 1 German naval hero.

Left: Christmas at the Anneke home, 1897. Right: Percy Anneke with his daughter, October 1896.

The Fitgers in the dining room at 629 East First Street in 1896. August, wife Clara, son Arnold, and daughters Wilhelmina and Marion.

The Annekes in the dining room of their Second Street home, October 1896. Percy's son Victor would be president of The Fitger Company during the Prohibition years.

in their town. Fitger's was most interested in the saloon, which was part of every hotel.

Fitger's real estate investments were not limited to hotels and saloons; the growing temperance movement had the company looking outside the brewery business. In Brainerd, Fitger's constructed a large brick building on the "Fitger Block." The Johnston Land Company, a part of Fitger's, platted the town site of Paine and constructed several commercial buildings, but the community never blossomed. Fitger's also owned lakeshore property on Lake Vermilion in Tower, Minnesota, and other potential mining and agricultural tracts.

Trouble Brewing

The prohibition movement had started in the middle of the nineteenth century and was originated and supported by women's groups. In the Duluth area, the first Temperance Society was organized in 1856 on the North Shore. In the 1800s, politicians listened to the prohibitionists' sentiments; because women didn't have the right to vote, however, they were not taken seriously. At one time the Prohibitionists actually had a candidate for President, but their strategy to spread the word from the top down was not successful.

Originally, beer and wine were not a concern for the Prohibitionists. As time went on, however, the prohi-

More of Fitger's real estate holdings: the Dowling and Pigott buildings in Virginia, Minnesota. Located on Chestnut Street, Virginia's main street, they were intended to be used for the construction of a "tied house," a saloon that would only dispense Fitger's beer.

bitionists targeted breweries because they felt the breweries had monopolistic control of the saloons and were not monitoring them properly.

The Anti-Saloon League—with the motto "The saloon must go"—developed in many cities because saloons were allowed widespread ordinance violations. These violations included selling beer to intoxicated people and allowing disruptive behavior in the saloons and adjacent public areas. When the Anti-Saloon League joined the Prohibition movement in the early twentieth century, their combined influence created greater momentum for change in liquor and beer laws.

While the prohibitionists were organized from the top down, the Anti-Saloon League started from the ground up. This grass roots strategy worked well in Minnesota. The Anti-Saloon League diligently investigated local laws and regulations and found a clause in some Indian treaties that prohibited the sale of liquor to the Native Americans. The League tried to use this provision to close down all saloons in any county that included Native American residents, even if the saloons did not serve Native Americans and none lived nearby.

This raised havoc in certain counties where Fitger's and other brewers had a lot of business, especially in the Bemidji and Cass Lake areas. Bureau of Indian Affairs agents went into the saloons without warning and told the managers they had to close the business within days. In one of his diaries, Fitger said, "This is what they do in Russia."

Even though the temperance movement continued to grow, brewers felt the government would never shut down

W. E. "Pussyfoot" Johnson

As a journalist, William E. Johnson had already been a crusader for the temperance movement for over fifteen years when, in 1906, he became a special officer in the Bureau of Indian Affairs, appointed by President Theodore Roosevelt. He went after the liquor traffic in Oklahoma with gusto, and was soon promoted to chief special liquor officer, with the job of curtailing the shipment and sale of intoxicating beverages in all Indian territories.

Agent Johnson would come in very quietly then suddenly accuse employees of violating the law and order them to close, usually within hours of his order. Because of his meek demeanor and misleading introductions, people referred to him as "Pussyfoot." Pussyfoot created a lot of problems for the brewers not only because of his abrasive tactics, but also because the breweries spent a lot of money for attorneys to protect their rights and investments.

Pussyfoot resigned in 1911. An article in a St. Paul newspaper reported, "Because his views regarding suppression of the liquor traffic among the Indians did not coincide with those of officials of the Federal Bureau of Indian Affairs, W. E. 'Pussyfoot' Johnson…famed from coast to coast and particularly in Minnesota, has resigned."

An editorial in the paper further stated, "'Pussyfoot' Johnson resigns. Pussyfoot Johnson, Agent of the Indian Bureau, who took advantage of a host of laws against selling liquor to Indians and imposed prohibition arbitrarily in the greater part of northern Minnesota has resigned and has stated as the reason the lack of accord between him and the department about how the law ought to be enforced. With all due respect to Mr. Johnson's earnestness and conscientiousness, his resignation was due. What he did in northern Minnesota was not to enforce the law as to protect the Indians from liquor but to take advantage of that law and obsolete treaties to impose prohibition on a large area most of which didn't contain a single Indian."

After resigning, Johnson joined the Anti-Saloon League, often traveling overseas on its behalf. He continued to travel around the world for the temperance movement until he retired in 1930. Johnson died in 1945.

the breweries because it would result in the loss of hundreds of millions of dollars in revenue annually. There was no federal income tax at the time; the main source of revenue for the federal government was the excise tax on so-called "luxury" items, including beer and liquor. While temporary income taxes had been imposed to finance the Civil War, national politicians considered them unconstitutional by the 1890s. State and local governments relied on personal property and real property taxes for revenue. But there was talk of amending the constitution to allow income tax.

In 1910, Fitger feared that the income tax amendment would soon become a reality and decided to be proactive. Fitger always had divorced the brewing of beer from the distillation of spirits during prohibition discussions. Fitger initiated an essay contest by placing ads in the *Duluth News-Tribune* explaining the good qualities of beer. He placed eight different ads over an eight-week period. Each ad discussed a topic and gave the reader information regarding that topic: 1) Feeding and eating; 2) Beverages and sociability; 3) The safety valve; 4) Beer,

New Stables and Garage

The final building Louis Lehle designed for Fitger's housed the new stables and garage. The $24,000 structure was at the foot of Fifth Avenue East and Michigan Street just below the railroad tracks. The old stables, built in 1899, were torn down to make room for the new structure.

The new stables were on the lowest level, with a garage on the main Michigan Street level and a carpenter shop above that. When the building was built in 1911, trucks were becoming the main mode of beer delivery. The stables were built so little renovation would be required to convert them into future garage space. (The building was torn down in the early 1980s as part of the I-35 extension.)

Driver Martin Jorstad in one of Fitger's first trucks, which could hold 100 cases of beer. The chain-drive flatbed was slow but powerful, and brewery mechanics were able to keep it in working order into the 1950s.

The Discussion Club

Fitger was an enthusiastic member of the Discussion Club. The members were considered to be some of Duluth's brightest businessmen. The club originally had eight members, each of whom prepared a lecture to be given during the eight months from September to April. Each of those months, the host would invite the other members to his home to listen to his lecture and discuss it afterwards. Fitger dedicated his 1910 lecture to Abraham Lincoln. In fact, Fitger admired Lincoln so much that even though the union contract at the brewery did not call for a holiday on Lincoln's Birthday, Fitger gave all employees a half-day off in Lincoln's honor.

The Discussion Club wasn't Fitger's only source of what would now be called "networking." The Kitchi Gammi Club, incorporated in 1883, was an all-male club founded by local businessmen including Guilford Hartley and Chester Congdon (who built the Glensheen estate) that drew its exclusive membership from prominent northeastern Minnesota businessmen. Both Fitger and Anneke joined the Kitchi Gammi Club after it built its present day site just a few blocks east of the Fitger's complex on Superior Street in 1913.

the temperance drink; 5) A lesson in nutrition; 6) Beer, the absolutely clean food; 7) What our beer is; and 8) Are drinking places necessary?

The ads requested readers to send in essays discussing each topic. At the end of the eight-week campaign, the author of the best essay received $50 in gold. A few years later, further public relations efforts to distinguish beer from distilled spirits in the prohibition debate failed.

Income Taxes Become Legal

In 1912, the United States Constitution was amended to allow the federal government to tax business and personal income. Now that the federal government could tax personal and business income to raise revenue to replace lost excise tax from breweries, brewers felt the government would be more apt to pass the prohibition laws that were gaining support throughout the United States. Obviously, this concerned Fitger and all brewers.

The two other breweries in Duluth had always depended on August Fitger to take the lead on whatever problems arose. One example of this was negotiation of labor contracts; it was always Fitger who would set the pattern and shoulder the responsibility of wages and contract wording. The others would follow. With the prohibition problem, the situation was the same. Fitger would be the leader.

Another Attempt to Diversify

Fitger and Anneke continued to diversify to protect their interests in case of prohibition. In 1912, they invested in a farming company known as the Silver Lake Farm. Located at Silver Lake, Wisconsin, the purpose of this farm was to raise registered animals, such as sheep and pigs, and also vegetables with the ultimate purpose of selling parcels of the land. Anneke and Fitger controlled approximately 1,500 acres of land and hired a professional farmer to manage the operation.

By 1915, the company had not turned a profit and the investors decided to sell. Interested buyers weren't able to pay the appraised value of the property, however, so eventually the investors leased the parcels out. (Hiram Elliott of Duluth, who owned Elliott Meats, was one of those lessees; Elliott Meats are still marketed, even though the plant closed in the early 1990s.) In 1924, it would be decided to finally dissolve Silver Lake Farm; the investors were forced to sell small parcels below the appraised values.

CHAPTER 9

Prohibition Approaches

In July 1913, a Duluth city commissioner proposed an ordinance to further control the sale of the liquor and beer. Rumors circled throughout the city that brewers, cigar makers (at the time there were more than one hundred cigar makers in Duluth), unions, and citizens would be opposed to the proposed ordinance. But Fitger, speaking for all the brewers in Duluth, told the newspaper, "It would be an easy matter to get one or two thousand people to send a petition and get a referendum, but it would do more harm than good. It would only irritate city commissioners, and, with their present means, they could simply lay new burdens on the trade in a hundred different ways."

The following day an editorial in the newspaper said, "August Fitger, head of the Fitger Brewing Company, speaking for that company and also for the other brewers, has said to the *News-Tribune* that they do not favor a referendum on the new liquor code and will discourage it. Mr. Fitger's word is good. No one in Duluth will question it."

Fitger's cynicism about the issue would soon receive further confirmation. In a March 17, 1914, diary entry, Fitger described a St. Paul meeting that brewery attorney Mr. Schmidt attended to hear former President and then-Supreme Court Justice William Howard Taft address the

Minnesota Supreme Court judges and district judges. "At banquet, cocktails were served, although it was an election day in St. Paul [all drinking establishments were closed on election day]. All Judges of Superior Court, countless District Judges present. On the same day at the St. Paul Hotel [several judges] ordered and paid for a bottle of whiskey, although it was Election Day. What hypocrisy!" That "blue" law continued through post-World War II days when it was finally repealed.

Quality Control Leads to Quality Investment

Fitger had started the first quality control laboratory in a Minnesota brewery in 1910, traveling to Germany to hire a chemist named von Sternberg, the son of baron, to head the new lab. Von Sternberg had brought all his own equipment with him from Germany, arriving in August 1910. While monitoring quality control and looking for improved methods for Fitger's products, von Sternberg became responsible for the largest and most successful investment Fitger and Anneke would ever undertake. Von Sternberg became aware of Kieselguhr, a company for sale near Santa Barbara, California, that mined diatomaceous earth. Diatomaceous earth was composed of decayed sea organisms piled in small mountains along the Pacific coast, where it had been deposited by wave action over tens of thousands of years. The diatomes were natural filtering agents and had many applications. Von Sternberg alerted his bosses to its availability, and Fitger and Anneke both went to California to visit the company. They thought it was a very good opportunity and met with a Duluth banker who felt they needed another partner to take on such a large venture. They tried unsuccessfully to find such a partner, then risked the investment themselves, which required a capitalization of nearly $2 million.

Fitger soon realized that diatomaceous earth, which was referred to by the company's name of Kieselguhr, would be an excellent filtering agent for beer. He became

the first brewer in the United States to use diatomaceous earth as a filter; Kieselguhr purified Fitger's beer without the use of steam. While Fitger's had always used only the best ingredients available and proven brewing methods, Fitger and Beerhalter felt this new process greatly improved the beer. So much, in fact, that it would lead to a new label. Meanwhile, von Sternberg went back to Germany, not returning to Duluth until late 1913.

A New Year's Day 1915 advertisement for the Kieselguhr filter and all the wonders that it brought to Fitger's beer, "The Most Brilliant Beer in America."

The chemist's small office included a workbench and all the necessary equipment for testing products at various stages of the brewing process and for testing new products Fitger's was developing. The chemist doubled as medical help if someone on the staff was injured.

Fitger's Introduces "Natural Beer"

The mainstay "Export Beer" label Fitger and Anneke had introduced in 1885 had been phased out after twenty-five years and replaced by the generic "Fitger's Beer" label. In 1914, with the advent of Beerhalter's patented Kieselguhr filtration process, Fitger's launched the "Natural Beer" label for its premium beer. Advertising stressed that Fitger's Natural Beer was not a "sweet" beer. One ad quoted master brewer John Beerhalter: "I never make a sweet beer. Real beer drinkers like the ones in Augsburg want a 'bite' to their beer. That's what gives you real refreshment."

The Kieselguhr filter became a huge financial success. Eventually, other breweries and wineries throughout the country used the Kieselguhr process of filtration. In addition to beverage filtering, it was also used as insulation for boilers and other machinery and eventually for filtration of swimming pools. (The swimming pool that the University of Minnesota Duluth built in 1953 used the process, a relatively new application for the Kieselguhr. It was lauded for producing water so pure that it was safe to drink even after people had swum in it.)

Prohibition Threat Causes New Strategies

Even with business booming, the prohibition movement continued to gain momentum and Fitger realized he better have an ace in the hole if he hoped to stay in business should prohibition become law. He started thinking about new products similar to the low alcohol beers served in the Scandinavian countries.

Von Sternberg had left Fitger Brewery in July 1914 to enlist in the German army; Germany entered World War I that August. Fitger had hired a new chemist, Charles Ringler. Fitger realized Ringler had some new brewing methods, especially for the forthcoming non-alcoholic beverages, so he agreed to pay Ringler $130 a month, more than von Sternberg. Fitger would receive one-half interest in any patents for processes that Ringler might develop during his Fitger's employment.

By 1916, Ringler and Master Brewer Beerhalter were granted two patents important to making nonalcoholic and low alcohol non-intoxicating beer. The new processes were featured in a national brewing publication and prompted inquiries from breweries across the nation. One of the new patents was designed specifically for Iowa, which forbade the use of any malt for near beer. Fitger patented and trademarked the name Non-Alco Beer and began marketing Non-Alco Beer using the Ringler and Beerhalter process before prohibition went into effect.

The laws of the surrounding states all varied in the amount of alcohol allowed in beer, with some districts allowing no more than two percent alcohol. Fitger's began

Top: The Fitger's Natural Beer label as introduced in 1914. The following year Fitger added the words "Kieselguhr Filtered." Bottom: Preparing for Prohibition.

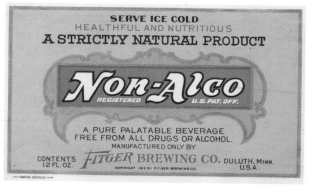

making a special two percent beer for North Dakota, called Dakota Beer, and a non-malt beverage for Iowa.

Fitger's also added Golden Common Sense, which was well-aged and only one to one-and-a-half percent alcohol. As Fitger stated in his diary, "This light beer was made of the choicest materials and was strictly non-intoxicating. It is much less alcoholic than the temperance beers fostered and favored by Scandinavian temperance societies and governments." John Beerhalter noted, "We often tapped some in our own saloon. The taste was so close to our regular beer that Fitger, himself, thought he was drinking regular beer."

Top: North Dakota's pre-Prohibition laws always were a little different from other states, so Fitger's brewed a beer specifically to meet those requirements. Bottom: Golden Common Sense was just under one-and-a-half percent alcohol.

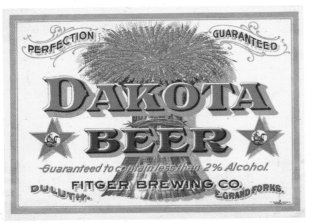

Fitger's had some problems with the non-alcoholic beer. It seemed that the taste of non-alcoholic beer changed from the time it was pasteurized to the time it was sold. After a lot of experimentation, Beerhalter determined that non-alcoholic beer needed to be pasteurized at a higher temperature and for a longer period of time than alcoholic beer. This solved the problem of taste deterioration, but non-alcoholic beer's popularity continued to decline because it was neither "near" nor "beer."

A New Brewery Saloon

Fitger's brewing and saloon business was booming in 1914, despite increased liquor controls in Duluth. Brewery Saloon sales were increasing and the saloon, even though it had been expanded twenty years earlier, was not large enough to accommodate the growing number of customers. The brewing operations in the original 1881 building were also outgrowing their space and needed to expand into the area that served as the Brewery Saloon. Because of these pressures, construction began for the new Brewery Saloon (which is the present site of the Pickwick) in June 1914.

Original plans called for a one-story building, but on June 6, 1914, it was decided to construct a two-story building. Anthony Puck of Duluth was selected as the architect.

Plans for the new saloon called for leaded glass imported from Belgium to be used throughout the new building. After war broke out in Europe, however, none of this material was available. Fitger's called on Saint Germain's Paint and Glass in Duluth to make arrangements with a company back East to manufacture the leaded glass, which still is in place at the Pickwick.

Some murals were transferred from the old Brewery Saloon. John Fery, one of the original Saloon's painters, painted the murals at the new Saloon. His former partner, Feodor von Leurzer, had been dead several years when these new murals were painted. Anneke imported the lion plaque for the new Brewery Saloon from Pompeii, Italy.

The last night of the old Brewery Saloon was on December 31, 1914. The new saloon opened on January 1, 1915. (From that date through the mid-1960s, most people believed there was a direct line pumping beer from the brewery to the saloon; brewery officials never questioned the rumor.) Fitger noted in his diary on December 31, "Tonight we closed our old saloon forever. It has been run for thirty-three years without an arrest or any complaint of any kind." A newspaper article written the following day stated, "Farewell to Old Landmark. Many 'hochs' resound for last time in Brewery Saloon. Many hochs and farewells were exchanged late last night at the famous old saloon in the Fitger Brewery addition that for many years has been a unique resort. The hochs were in celebration for the death of 1914 and the advent of 1915, and because it was the last night in the old place, a number of old patrons sang appropriate songs. Today the new saloon nearby was opened. All of the pictures in the old place were removed to the new one and at eleven P.M. the key was turned into the lock."

Murals from the Brewery Saloon, now in the Pickwick. Originally commissioned by August Fitger in 1914, they include a depiction of Fitger's boyhood home in Delmenhorst, Germany. The post office is on the left, the hotel in the center.

Prohibition Movement Targets Beer, Too

While the original prohibition movement had targeted "demon rum," or whiskey, Fitger was concerned that beer was now becoming a major target of the prohibition movement. He believed the war in Europe and the growing anti-German sentiments would make this even worse

Top: Custom-designed glass from 1914 is still in its original place at the Pickwick.

Bottom: The bar back constructed for the old Brewery Saloon was moved to the new Brewery Saloon, and remains in the Pickwick to this day.

because most brewers were of German descent and beer was seen as a German-inspired product. World War I eventually involved many countries, and most of these countries' newspapers felt Germany, rather than Britain, was the aggressor. The writers lashed out at Germany through their editorials and stories. When German submarines sank the *Lusitania* in 1915, it furthered the anti-German sentiment throughout America.

Most Germans living in America, including Fitger, would never, absolutely never, talk about the European situation for fear that there would be repercussions. In his diary Fitger lamented, "If the national drink of the American people had been beer and the Germans had come into the country bringing and introducing whiskey, then and in that case, the German would and should have been kicked out, whiskey and all. But the shoe fits the other foot. And before the American will admit that he was wrong and the German was right, he will kick out whiskey and beer both."

Beginning of the End

In 1915 the Minnesota State Legislature passed the County Option bill, allowing Minnesota counties and larger cities to vote on the issue of whether to remain "wet" or become "dry." The brewery's economic boom ended abruptly as prohibitionists gained more popularity. In 1916, barrelage at Fitger's dropped nearly twenty-five percent from the previous year. Fitger's Natural Beer sales also dropped dramatically. Sales of Non-Alco and Golden Common Sense increased somewhat, but not nearly enough to offset the decreases in regular beer.

Part III

The Prohibition Years

Fitger's Brewery in the 1920s.

CHAPTER 10

Prohibition Arrives Early

Duluth voted dry in April 1917 and the law went into effect on July 1, 1917. Two Harbors, Lake County, and Carlton County went dry the same year. Then Saint Louis County also voted dry in September 1917, effective in March 1918. Adding to any breweries' difficulties, the federal government, with the entrance into World War I, doubled the excise tax on beer from $1.50 to $3 a barrel to help pay for America's war effort. In November 1917, Charles Ringler, head of Fitger's quality control, left the brewery to accept a job as brewmaster at a brewery in Fort William, Canada. He got a $50 a month pay increase, to $180, and was able to brew real beer. A replacement would not be hired until the late 1920s when John Hey started at the brewery. He was a pharmacist who had lost his license for selling "medicinal" materials during Prohibition. (Hey retired in the mid-1960s and after that the brewmaster absorbed his duties.)

Duluth Celebrates Last Day of Public Drinking

The last day the saloons would be open was June 30, 1917, which happened to fall on a Saturday. Thousands of people turned out in downtown Duluth to be part of this last night of revelry. At ten o'clock in the evening, the saloons would lock their doors and Duluth would become a "dry" city. Sixty-nine saloons were affected and about three hundred male bartenders became unemployed.

The *Duluth News-Tribune* and the *Duluth Herald* gave this event significant coverage. One of the headlines read, "Festive Scenes Attend End of John Barleycorn, Pioneer." Another stated, "Duluth is Dry for the First Time in its History."

Few women participated in the last night drinking spree. The only place women could legally be served any alcoholic beverages—beer, wine, or liquor—was in a hotel lounge. A city ordinance not allowing ladies to be served in a bar was in effect until the early 1950s. The more sophisticated clientele appeared at hotels with their wives or girlfriends while the bachelors hit the saloons. One reporter stated, "The triangle, that is, wine, women and song, didn't apply to either group as the hotel crowd felt it was below their dignity to sing while the saloon crowd saw the absence of women but they imbibed in a lot of wine and song."

The Cloquet–Moose Lake Fire of 1918

The Cloquet–Moose Lake Fire was actually about a half-dozen separate major forest fires and several other smaller fires that ravaged northeastern Minnesota on October 12, 1918. It covered approximately 1,500 square miles, killed more than 450 people, and burned over a dozen towns and villages to the ground—including Cloquet and Moose Lake—while severely damaging another two dozen. The fire that burned through Cloquet was the largest of the fires, burning as far west as Floodwood, north beyond Brookston and Twig, and east into Lakewood just north of Duluth. Many of those fleeing the fire found refuge in Duluth's National Guard Armory.

The brewery donated its wagons and horses to help transfer the many people who were burned out of their homes and farms in Lakewood. All told, approximately 52,000 people had been injured or displaced by the fires. The Red Cross in Duluth arranged for the courthouse, the Shrine auditorium, the Masonic temple, various YMCA buildings, and many churches and hotels to shelter the influx of refugees. The people of Duluth also opened their homes to fire survivors.

The fire's path spared August Fitger's Lakewood farm, Elmhurst, but a Fitger's Brewery warehouse alongside a railroad line in Cloquet burned to the ground along with the rest of the city. Fitger's eventually collected $500 from insurance on the building.

Not all who visited the saloons on that Saturday night were drinkers. Abstainers came out in numbers due to curiosity and to see who was in the crowd. Many white-collar men who frequented the main street saloons or hotel bars ventured into the old-time bowery areas of the city because their usual haunts were too crowded for them to get waited on. It truly became a mix of people from all walks of life that night before Prohibition. Just before

closing up, many of the saloons held auctions to sell glasses, rare wines, and whiskeys, some of which had not been seen in a quarter of a century. By ten o'clock, when all the patrons left the saloons, it looked like a typical Christmas shopping day as many people were carrying packages. Most of the people were carrying these packages by the neck of a bottle. And perhaps surprisingly to the prohibitionists, it was a very orderly drinking fest, according to the police department. Police Captain Fiskett noted, "Never have I seen the equal of the drinking tonight after touring Superior Street."

Superior Votes Wet

Across the St. Louis River from Duluth, the city of Superior, Wisconsin, also voted on the wet/dry question, but those voters elected to keep selling beer and liquor. Fitger's still had a source of business across the bay and now concentrated on selling beer to saloons and private customers in the Superior area.

At first, Fitger's used what appeared to be a loophole in the law to provide beer to its private customers in Duluth. Although it was illegal to sell beer from the brewery to customers in Duluth, Fitger's established a Fitger agency in Superior. Duluth customers could call Fitger's in Duluth and request delivery of beer from the Wisconsin agency, which Fitger's arranged if the beer was prepaid prior to delivery. Eventually, this process was determined to be a violation of the law and Duluthians had to cross the bridge themselves to pick up beer from Superior. Without the advantage of delivery, Duluthians were no longer loyal to the Fitger's brand, so again sales suffered. By the latter part of 1918 and into early 1919, Fitger's was selling beer only on a contractual basis to Hamm's Brewing Company in Saint Paul, which was not yet affected by Prohibition.

Prohibitionists continued to push for local prohibition in parts of Minnesota that had not voted dry, and used World War I as an additional justification. The State

Winter Recreation

Not all the Fitger's recreation occurred in the summer months. John Hey noted that many winter activities took place behind Fitger's on Lake Superior, including curling, horse and cutter races, skating races, iceboat races, and an annual winter carnival.

John Beerhalter was one of the old-timers who started curling at a private home in Duluth Heights. The only members of this curling group who had automobiles were John Beerhalter and Max W. Wirth, a druggist whose building still stands 13 West Superior Street. The other members were architect George Wirth (Max Wirth's brother), civil engineer Louis A. Berg, Jim Berg, realtor Otto Leland, and carpenters Carl Kogol, G. Klatz, and Joe Donaher.

If they didn't get a ride with Beerhalter or Worth, they had to take the Incline Railway from Seventh Avenue West and Superior Street to the top of the hill and then transfer to the Highland Avenue and Swan Lake Road trolley route, which was nicknamed the Toonerville Trolley, after a comic strip in the newspaper. Almost every Sunday the group would meet at Louis Berg's house in Duluth Heights. He was a bachelor who had a long, 150-foot driveway. The Duluth Fire Department charged $3 to flood the driveway each year.

Top: The Incline Railway. Bottom: Curling on Lake Superior.

Prohibition Goes National

The resolution to submit the Prohibition Amendment to the states for ratification passed in 1917 after receiving the required two-thirds majority vote in Congress. A temporary Wartime Prohibition Act was also passed during World War I to save grain for food. The war ended in 1918, but on January 29, 1919, the Eighteenth Amendment was ratified.

It was to go into effect one year later, and by January 1920 thirty-three states were already living under prohibition. The National Prohibition Act, providing guidelines for enforcing prohibition, had passed on October 28, 1919. It was known as the Volstead Act, after Congressman Andrew J. Volstead, its chief promoter.

Safety Commission, the name for the political arm of the prohibition movement, took out ads stating, "Wartime Prohibition. Minnesota will save thousands of tons of coal, millions of bushels of grain. In six months, according to *The Western Brewer*, Minnesota has consumed in the manufacture of beer 99,980 tons of coal and 967,551 bushels of edible grain. Patriotic Americans desire to conserve fuel, grain, men and help the transportation problem."

In fact, Minnesota businesses were conserving coal to assist in the war movement and Fitger's was no exception. Fitger's Brewery had "Heatless Monday" when the entire brewery operation was closed to conserve coal. Brewing non-alcoholic "near beer" did not conserve grain since the brewing process consumed as much grain per barrel as regular beer—the only difference was the yeast. The continued propaganda and other efforts by the prohibition movement were finally successful and all of Minnesota was dry many months before national prohibition went into effect in 1920.

Annekes Take Control at Fitger's

Amid the turmoil during 1917 and 1918, Anneke started thinking about having his son join him full-time in the brewing business. Anneke was living in Duluth year round, while August Fitger spent the majority of his time handling the Kieselguhr business in California.

Anneke's son, Victor, who had entered Cornell University in Ithaca, New York, had been involved in a serious motorcycle accident. Anneke spent significant time back East during his son's recuperation, and then Victor started working intermittently at Fitger's in 1918.

Fitger's son Arnold, who graduated from the University of Wisconsin at Madison in 1914, had worked at the brewery for a couple years after graduation and then for the Kieselguhr Company before returning to Duluth to enlist in the Army. After serving in the trenches in Europe and surviving without injury, Arnold returned to Kieselguhr. He enjoyed the big city life in New York and Los Angeles and did not appear interested in working at the brewery in Duluth.

Anneke proposed that Fitger buy out Anneke's shares in Kieselguhr Company and, in turn, Anneke would buy enough of Fitger's stock to become majority owner. They finalized the transaction in 1918. Fitger, now a minority stockholder, still spent several months every winter and several months every summer in Duluth, offering counsel to the Annekes on business issues. Fitger also hired a new chauffeur, Richard Kohtz, a native German who Fitger found dependable and trustworthy. As part of his pay, Kohtz was provided a rent-free house half a block from the brewery, next to the Beerhalter home, also owned by Fitger.

Under Anneke, the Fitger Brewing Company changed its name to The Fitger Company; after all, it was no longer in the beer-brewing business. The Fitger Company was an umbrella corporation with smaller entities for beverage production, real estate, and, later, candy, soft drink, and cigar sales. With all the problems confronting the brewery and the anti-German feelings of World War I, Fitger and Anneke purchased more than $30,000 in Liberty Bonds.

Victor married Elsa Krause in Saint Louis, Missouri, on May 10, 1919. The Krause family was a very close friend of Adolphus Busch, who sold Busch the label "Budweiser." The Busch family attended the wedding. Charles Krause, Victor's father-in-law, would become an important adviser to Victor.

Fitger's Starts Slowly with Soft Drinks

The brewery business was changing when Anneke purchased controlling interest in The Fitger Company in 1918. The biggest question facing breweries was whether they could adjust from a brewery to a manufacturer and jobber of other products. Many breweries decided not to try to make the change and just closed their doors. Some tried to adjust but closed their doors after a few years. Anneke believed repeal of Prohibition would come much earlier than it did, and Fitger's was one of the very few brewers in the entire country that remained open throughout Prohibition.

Anneke launched a soft drink business as soon as he took over leadership and majority ownership control at Fitger's. The Colonel's Choice label was developed solely for Northern Drug Company in Duluth. Fitger's also had a private label for Gershgol's food markets. The brewery contracted various soft drinks to different companies, mostly in the wholesale grocery business.

Non-Alco was not selling well, and Golden Common Sense had to be taken off the market completely, because the maximum alcohol content for Prohibition beer was no more than 0.05 percent. In order to keep as many employees working as possible and to keep machinery in productive use, Fitger's set up an operation in part of the bottle house to make soft drinks in bulk.

Since Ringler had left, John Beerhalter had assumed responsibility for both beer and soft drink production, along with managing the facility. Beerhalter noted later,

Soda pop bottle circa 1918. Most soft drinks, however, were still sold by the glass at drugstore counters.

"This made a long day for me, twelve to fifteen hours, seven days a week. At the time, we started making soft drinks, at first in bulk, in our bottle house." Most soft drinks were dispensed by the glass at drugstore counters and were not a significant retail commodity. It would be several years before Fitger's committed to the production of soft drinks and candy on a large scale.

Fitger's Makes Other Changes

Fitger's decided to give up direct control of the Brewery Saloon in 1918, although the company still owned the building and all its fixtures and also continued a relationship to other "tied houses." Joe Wisocki Sr., the manager of the Brewery Saloon and employee of Fitger's, was taken off the Fitger's payroll and began leasing the building from Fitger's. The Brewery Saloon continued to serve only Fitger's products and most patrons referred to the saloon as just plain "Fitger's."

When the brewery launched its famous Pickwick non-alcoholic beverage in 1919, it was an immediate success and continued to be so throughout the Prohibition years. Brewery Saloon customers kept asking

Beerhalter (second from right) and others in the second floor rec room of the new office building, circa 1920. At the far right is Richard Kohtz, August Fitger's chauffeur.

for "Pickwick." Soon customers started referring to the tavern itself as "Pickwick." Eventually, the name was formally changed to Pickwick, and it remains the Pickwick today.

Because of Prohibition, ice was no longer needed for tavern customers, so ice harvesting was discontinued. The ice house became a general storage area, mostly for storing empty beer bottles and cases. It could hold up to 40,000 cases with room to spare. Eventually the ice house was demolished, and the property sold in the late 1960s. With no new fixtures required for taverns, fewer carpenters were needed. When six carpenters told the head carpenter, Joe Ario, they would quit unless they received an increase in wages equal to carpenter wages under the Duluth Area Building and Construction Trades Council contract, Fitger told Ario, "Let them terminate their services." That eliminated the headache of laying them off. Later, Carl Leland asked if he could be reinstated, and he was.

The drop in beer sales and the use of beer trucks meant another change. In 1919, Fitger noted in his diary, "Eleven horses are in the barn. No need for work so they're leased out to other businesses in town."

A label for Pickwick, a non-alcoholic beverage that changed the Brewery Saloon's name. With Prohibition, the saloon could no longer serve beer. The Pickwick beverage became so popular customers started referring to the saloon itself as "The Pickwick." Brewery Saloon bartender Joseph S. Wisocki took over operation the establishment prior to Prohibition and turned it into one of Duluth's favorite restaurants. His grandsons operate the business today.

One of Fitger's early chain-driven trucks on the new cobblestones of Superior Street.

Chapter 11

From Father to Son

On January 12, 1920, August Fitger noted in his diary, "Old Bottling House and Saloon badly gutted by fire. Insurance $2,500 on the building, $500 on the contents." The morning newspaper on Tuesday reported the fire:

Fire Destroys Original Unit of Fitger Brewery

The original Fitger brewery on East Superior street, built in 1882 by August Fitger, was gutted by fire of unknown origin which broke out at 10 o'clock last night and burned until nearly midnight. The main plant was unharmed by the blaze which called out most of the fire departments.

The old brewery and saloon structure stood between the two massive stone and brick buildings that house the brewery proper on the one hand, and the office and bottling department on the other. It was of heavy frame construction with a front of brick veneer.

Founder Recalls Labors

"I put those bricks in place with my own hands nearly 40 years ago," said Mr. Fitger, founder of the brewery, as he watched the blaze.

One part of the building in former days was used as a saloon, the other part for the manufacture of liquors. It was a landmark on the lake front when it was erected.

Flames Rise High

Of recent years the building has been used for the storage of cases, bottles, barrels and advertising matter. Three hundred light barrels in one section of the building sent flames high above the four-story modern brewery which the old building adjoins. Firemen put six streams of water on the building from the roof and front windows.

Mr. Fitger said he would be unable to estimate the loss until the ruins cool. The greatest loss, he said, would be on advertising matter, practically all of which was stored in the structure.

Fitger's quote—"I put those bricks in place with my own hands nearly forty years ago"—was a bit of poetic license; the original brewery, begun in 1881, had already been completed by Fink early in 1882 and producing beer for months before Fitger arrived.

No foul play was suspected. The abundant fuel made the fire extremely difficult to control. The paper and cardboard advertising materials and the wooden barrels were stored in the building because it was no longer needed for brewing operations, and the original Brewery Saloon had been replaced by the new saloon, now called the Pickwick. The adjoining buildings to the original 1881 structure—the office building on the east and the brew house on the west—were essentially fireproof because they had been built with stone as thick as eighteen inches, providing a firewall between the old frame and brick structure and the newer buildings.

Family Tragedy

On the following day, January 13, 1920, Fitger's daughter Marion died suddenly. He was devastated and wrote in his diary (translated from German): "Now bow before the unchanging law of the way of things and pull yourself up to your old manhood to master your pain. Learn to rid yourself of the thought that you are only destined to happiness. And learn to bear your pain for the world is full of pain." The newspaper account read in part:

MARION FITGER DIES SUDDENLY.

Daughter of Prominent Duluth Businessman succumbs to Brief Illness. Miss Marion Fitger, age 23, youngest daughter of Mr. and Mrs. August Fitger, died yesterday after a brief illness. Miss Fitger was popular among Duluth's younger set. She was one of the King's Daughter's. She had been ill for but three days, death occurring from tubercular meningitis. Miss Fitger attended National Cathedral School in Washington and Miss Chamberlain's School in Boston, specializing in music.

Fitger went to Milwaukee for Marion's burial in the family plot and stayed there for two weeks. During this time he grieved deeply and did not write in his business journal. He returned to the brewery only briefly before going home to California and did not return to Duluth until May.

Some months after the fire, Fitger and Anneke considered replacing the two-story building with a substantial structure between the office building and the brew house. The cost estimates were high and their bankers suggested caution—Prohibition was in effect expanding the soft drink business and starting other non-brewery businesses would require capital. Fitger and Anneke took the advice of the bankers, cleared away the rubble, and built a one-story structure on the old foundation. Cream-colored brick was

The one-story structure (left) which replaced the old brewery building.

salvaged from the ruins and reused for the facade on the Superior Street side of the building. The new structure was still used for advertising and storage, but in a few years it would house the Silver Spray Gym. This area, now the main entrance from Superior Street to the Fitger's Retail Complex, is on the foundation that is the oldest part of the Fitger's Brewery Complex, dating back to 1881.

The Next Generation Takes the Reins

On April 20, 1920, just three months after the fire, Victor Anneke became president of The Fitger Company. Although he had worked at the brewery only part-time for two years, his father, Percy, was ready to pass on his legacy. Victor was not left without guidance, however, as his father and August Fitger were constant and close advisors.

Victor was taking over a business facing constant financial pressures. Early in 1921, Fitger's reduced salaries of office employees by fifteen percent. The pay for the rest of the employees stayed the same, as they were bound by a union contract. The strategy to keep the business alive, however, did require allocating capital to increase sales of Fitger's products. With sales volume for Non-Alco stagnant, new products were developed in order to try to stimulate interest in the non-intoxicating beers, limited by Prohibition to less than one-half percent alcohol. The

most popular brand by far was Pickwick; later, Fitger's added the Town Club and Dog's Head labels to the new Pickwick brand, which all fared much better on the market than the Non-Alco brand.

Anneke still hoped that Prohibition would be repealed quickly and did not allow the physical plant to deteriorate. Fitger's modernized the bottle house during the early 1920s by installing a new skid system, a new pas-

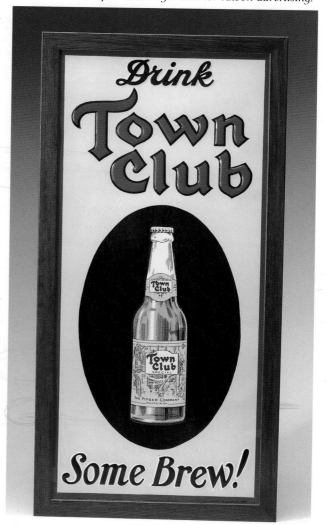

A Town Club stamped metal sign used for saloon advertising.

The Dog's Head Lager label. The neck label also featured the bulldog.

Fitger's Picnics are a Big Hit

Vic Anneke started annual picnics in 1921. Prior to 1917, all three Duluth breweries held combined annual picnics, but these were suspended when the United States entered World War I in 1917 and were not revived after the war ended. The pre-war picnics had been held at Fond du Lac, an old trading post, reachable only by railroad or boat. Getting to the Fitger's picnics in the 1920s was a major excursion as well.

Fitger's transported the employees and their families by automobile to the first annual picnic at Elmhurst, Fitger's country estate in Lakewood. The first picnic honored the women in the office. For many of the workers and their children, the trip to the picnic was their first automobile ride; automobiles were still a rarity for the average person. Fitger's furnished both an afternoon lunch and a supper at the picnics, as well as constant activities until dusk. At the first picnic, Joe Wisocki catered a beef dinner for everyone. The festivities did not end at sundown, however. The women from the office received permission to use the salesman's room on the third floor of the office building, which had a hardwood floor, and they danced into the night.

Many of the later, all-employee picnics were held at the Duluth Automobile Club on Pike Lake, located outside Duluth. Like the earlier picnics, caravans of cars were used. The car motors were not as strong as today, so the grade up Mesaba Avenue all the way to the Miller Trunk was much too steep for automobiles with any amount of people in them. The caravan followed a westerly route from Fitger's to Mesaba Avenue, then up the grade only to Second Street, then east on Second Street until Sixth Avenue East. Now they were just two blocks north of where they had started. The caravan followed Sixth Avenue East up to the Miller Trunk to the Midway Road, and then turned right for two blocks to the Auto Club.

The picnics were very organized. The program from a picnic at the Auto Club provides an example. Each individual received a typewritten form listing the time of each event. The various activities included races and contests, a baseball game between workers in the bottle house and the office, recreational swimming, and swimming races, as well. Winners of each event would receive various prizes from chocolates to cigars. The grand prize was given for finding a green ball hidden somewhere on the premises. Signs noted, "Look for the Green Ball" or "Keep your eyes open."

Employees pose at the east end of the bottle house to commemorate the first Fitger's picnic in 1921. This picnic was only for the office employees; the following year the picnic was for all employees.

Employees pose in front of Fitger's prior to the automobile ride to the first all-employee picnic, August 14, 1922.

Company picnic at the Duluth Automobile Club on Pike Lake.

teurizer, and new filters. Fitger's also kept some tied houses open during Prohibition to sell their products. They knew business would be down substantially, so Fitger's made their bars shorter. They felt a full short bar was better than a long bar only half full.

Candy and Soft Drinks
Help Fill the Beer Gap

Victor Anneke wanted to keep as many employees as possible working at Fitger's, but the beer product sales alone could not justify the employment level. In order to retain employees, he decided to get into soft drink, candy, and cigar manufacturing and distributing. Fitger's network of distributors was ready made for this new venture. August Fitger and Percy Anneke had set out the strategy several years earlier in order to keep the brewery open throughout Prohibition, which they truly expected to last only a short time.

In October 1921, Fitger's agreed to purchase a Duluth candy company from two Greek immigrants who had filed for bankruptcy, Mr. Pappas and Mr. Chickers

(Chickers is the short, Americanized version of a longer Greek name). Percy Anneke and August Fitger were trustees of the company until they could complete the incorporation of their own company, Purity Candy Company.

Within the first pay period, dissension occurred. Mr. Pappas and Mr. Chickers felt that their paychecks should be $50 each. Vic Anneke had already written out the checks for $35. Both Pappas and Chickers maintained they were working too hard, so they should get the same weekly pay as the other candy makers in town. Anneke then told them, "That's exactly what happened to your business. You were taking too high salaries and you weren't making enough money. However, let's let this ride and at the next pay period, maybe we can settle something out." The trustees paid them $35 again the next week. Pappas felt he should get $50. Chickers said he worked fifteen hours a day and would quit rather than work for $35. So Anneke compromised with them and paid Mr. Pappas $45 and Chickers $40 for the week. This rate of pay lasted for several weeks, during which time the earnings in the candy factory

The Town Club labels. Town Club had wide distribution beyond the regular Fitger's territory.

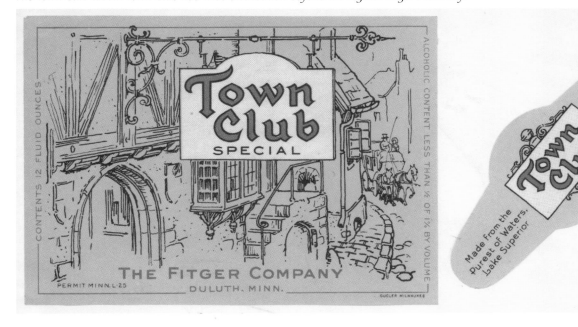

decreased. When their pay was reduced further to $30 and $25 a week, respectively, Pappas and Chickers gave two weeks notice. Acting for the Purity Candy Company, Anneke paid Pappas and Checkers $900 a piece to settle the situation. Now the Purity Candy Company belonged solely to Fitger's. Changes were on the way.

At this time, most candies were sold in the store by the pound or the box. Always on top of marketing innovations and trends, Fitger's recognized that the new individually wrapped candy bars would become more popular and introduced a number of candy bars, all under the name of Fitger's. The ten-cent candy bars were Fitger's Big Boy, Cherry Dips, and Nut Goodies.

The five-cent candy bars included Fitger's Arrowhead, Charleston, Nut Goodies (smaller version), Snow Cap, Kewpie Bar, Ping Pong, Polly-O, Skookum, Wonder Bar, Blue Bird, King Bee, Bon-Bon, Puddle Jumper, East Wind, Spark Plug, Little Boy, and a host of others. Fitger's also packaged specialty candies for holiday and seasonal promotions. Fitger's Cherry Egg was to be a five-cent version of the ten-cent Cherry Dips, but was never introduced.

Candy sales steadily increased for several years. For the first nine months of 1923, candy sales amounted to $159,000. But candy was not profitable for Fitger's. John Beerhalter wrote, "We lost money in big quantities. We bought jellybeans by the carload and sold them below cost to avoid spoiling. With advertising, it was the same. Bought in large quantities and when it went out-of-date burned half of it under the boiler. There was pilfering of chocolate in big slabs. We found at one time about half a ton under the driveway behind the wash house. The loss was so large that we discontinued the operation." Employees did get some free candy legally, however. When candy was cut to size, they could take the trimmings. Besides making their own candy, Fitger's also distributed national brands—Curtis Candies, Snickers, Milky Way, Luden's, Smith Brothers Cough Drops, Wrigley and Yucatan gums, and others.

Have a Cigar

In addition to candy, Fitger's also distributed cigars made by other companies. Cigar sales for the first nine months of 1923 amounted to $36,000, less than one-quarter the sales for candy. The Fitger Company originally started out with the El Verso cigar, but eventually took on the distribution of the El Producto, the Garcia Grande, and several other five cent cigars, all national brands; the Dan Patch, a regional cigar; and the ten-cent and fifteen-cent

Top: In the spring of 1921, Fitger's soda pop and cider labels had a dull, greenish-yellow background rather than the traditional gold background, but still had the SS Duluth *in the red star.*

Bottom: A brighter label was introduced in the summer of 1921, with the traditional gold background of Fitger's beer labels and a white background for the pop flavor to make it easier to read.

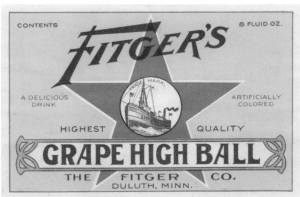

El Coro cigars, made by the Duluth Cigar Company until the early 1950s.

These additional products contributed to overall sales, but the beverage department still accounted for most of the business for the brewery. The Fitger Company had sixty-six distributors in the states of Minnesota, Wisconsin, Michigan, Iowa, and North and South Dakota. In 1923, 302 railroad cars were loaded to the various destinations.

In 1923, Fitger's employed eighty-five people. Four were the officers, August Fitger, Percy Anneke, Victor Anneke, and P.C. Schmidt, the attorney. John Beerhalter and Joe Polski acted as superintendents. The remaining seventy-eight worked in various divisions: eighteen in the office; seventeen as salesmen; six in the bottling department; eleven at the Pickwick company; five in the warehouse; seven at Purity Candy; and fifteen under the Fitger Company. In addition to being in charge of the various clerical responsibilities for Fitger's, the office staff handled the real estate of the Johnstown Company.

The pressures on Victor Anneke, who had been Fitger's president for only three years, continued to mount.

Labels for various candies produced by the Fitger company. Fitger's Cherry Egg (bottom right) was to be a five-cent version of the company's ten-cent Cherry Dips, but was never introduced.

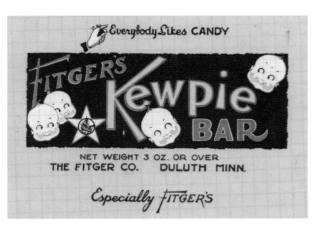

CHAPTER 12

Soda Pop

Fitger's was one of the first breweries in the country to start dispensing carbonated soft drinks by the bottle. The company started producing their own line of flavored beverages in six-ounce glass bottles embossed with the word "Fitger" and the Fitger's star. Fitger's used its existing distribution network for sale of the new beverages.

The soft drinks featured myriad flavors that often changed. In addition to the usual flavors of grape, orange and strawberry, Fitger's bottled Imitation Chocolate Milk Shake, Black Calf, Black Cow, Imitation Cherry Flip, Ginger Ale, Grape High Ball, Lemon Soda, Lime Rickey, Raspberry Punch, Strawberry Fizz, and Carbonated Water. Fitger's was still experimenting with different ingredients, hoping for that one special beverage that would be accepted by the public and make some money for the company.

Victor Anneke Assumes More Responsibilities

Percy Anneke suffered a paralytic stroke on December 31, 1923. After spending several months in a sanitarium in Battle Creek, Michigan, he moved to California to spend the remaining years of his life under the care of his daughter. Victor was well-prepared to handle his growing responsibilities with the continuing counsel of August Fitger and also his father-in-law, Charles Krause, who was a successful businessman in St. Louis.

In 1924, however, August Fitger was spending more time in California, looking after the Celite Corporation (formerly Kieselguhr) and his other interests. He kept modernizing the Celite plant and expanding markets worldwide. The newspaper in Santa Barbara reported, "In the past few years, this company has demonstrated unusual earning power, profits of about $34,000 in 1916 being increased to

Fitger's and The Real Thing

As Fitger's entered the soda pop market, a few national soft drink brands had already emerged, including Coca-Cola, one of the most popular fountain drinks in America since the late 1890s. Tom Moore, who formerly sold brewery equipment and was acquainted with August Fitger, owned the Coca-Cola franchise for the Upper Midwest. He knew Fitger's had an excellent distribution network and offered Fitger the Coca-Cola territory for Duluth, Two Harbors, and Cloquet. The franchise agreement required the brewery to purchase Coke bottles, cases, and all the syrup from Tom Moore. Fitger felt the investment was too large and didn't like the syrup arrangement either, so, as he had done with the 3M investment opportunity nearly twenty years earlier, he said "Nit" to the project. If Fitger had taken the Coca-Cola franchise, the history of Fitger's may have changed dramatically.

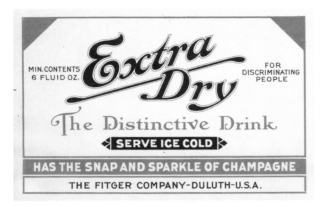

Above: The 1924 Extra Dry label.

Below: Out back of the brewery, 1924.

$347,000 in 1923. Average earnings for the past five years before depreciation have exceeded seven times dividend requirements on this stock while for 1922 and the first three months of 1923, they have been at the rate of twelve times dividends of the first preferred [stock]."

John Beerhalter, who always had been a trusted employee of August Fitger and Percy Anneke, now became Victor Anneke's trusted assistant and friend.

Extra Dry—A Success Story Begins

Years of experimentation led Fitger's to test market a new beverage. Extra Dry was launched in 1924 with advertise-

ments in the *Duluth News-Tribune*, the *Duluth Herald*, and in the program of the Orpheum Theater, the largest theater in town at that time. The advertising touted, "Extra Dry, the new distinctive drink, has the taste and sparkle of champagne."

Extra Dry was an immediate success and the Fitger Company decided that this was what they had been seeking—a distinctive product. Originally, Fitger's purchased extract from a Glenwood, Minnesota, business, with a provision that no other bottler received the same extract. Fitger's eventually learned that the Glenwood firm was furnishing the same extract to another bottler in southeastern Minnesota. John Beerhalter started developing his own recipe so the contract could be terminated. Beerhalter recalled later, "At the start, we bought fully mixed syrup in wooden barrels. It took me about a year to work out an extract of our own. By saving barrels, freight and handling, we cut the cost to less than half."

Above: A newspaper advertisement for Silver Spray, touted as "NOT a Ginger Ale."

Below: Silver Spray body and neck labels.

"Silver Spray is NOT a Ginger Ale"

Fitger's started plans for selling the new beverage beyond Fitger's usual distribution territory. Management was also trying to develop a different name for the product that would give it a better identity. Within a few months, they created a new label called "Silver Spray." Fitger's created a major promotional campaign and formally launched Silver Spray in Duluth on July Fourth, 1925.

The advertising slogans, "The taste and sparkle of champagne," "The best mixer in the crowd," and "Silver Spray is NOT a Ginger Ale" suggested this was more than a soft drink. The crown of the bottle was even covered with silver foil. The neck label read, "For Discriminating People." Foregoing the usual Fitger's logo, a new stylized shield with TFC (The Fitger Company) monogram was created. In anticipation of widespread distribution beyond Fitger's normal territory, the label said "Duluth-U.S.A."

Because Silver Spray was caramel-based and therefore light gold in color, people could mix it with colorless moonshine and ice cubes to achieve the appearance of a pre-Prohibition drink. Silver Spray would be Fitger's most popular and widespread product ever.

The bottle house in mid-1920s, bottling Silver Spray.

Silver Spray Sales Spread Quickly

The instant popularity encouraged Fitger's to increase the advertising budget and begin marketing Silver Spray in Minneapolis. Shortly after the first carload of Silver Spray arrived in Minneapolis, distribution spread to Chicago and Texas—Silver Spray was on its way to becoming a national drink. Fitger's set up a special office for Silver Spray in Chicago. Eventually, Silver Spray was sold in thirty-one states. Silver Spray never did break into the east coast market, but it spread to the west coast. The delivery route of Silver Spray to San Francisco was interesting; rather than ship it by railroad directly from Duluth to San Francisco, it was cheaper to send it by train to New York or Philadelphia, load it on a boat, and ship it through the Panama Canal to San Francisco.

Phenomenal growth and success of Silver Spray soon required Fitger's to purchase additional equipment to keep up with the demand. John Beerhalter said, "We sold all over the U.S. in large quantities and were falling behind in production. I was sent out to buy another unit and found one at the Cook Brewing Company in Evansville, Indiana."

Additional employees were also hired at Fitger's. National marketing expertise was needed and Thomas Miller became secretary-treasurer of the Fitger Company, replacing Percy Anneke, who had become incapacitated after a stroke. Miller had sixteen years experience as an executive with the Marshall Welles Company, a nationwide hardware distribution company. Victor Anneke also hired a new sales and advertising manager for Silver Spray, J. S. Lamb. Anneke had surrounded himself with a competent crew to expand the distribution of Silver Spray.

Promotion of Silver Spray in the Minnesota-Wisconsin area received special attention, however. It was not limited to newspaper and theater advertising. Fitger's used many creative marketing gimmicks to advertise the new product. Shortly after launching Silver Spray, Fitger's hired a seaplane to drop 15,000 leaflets over Duluth extolling the "goodness" of the new beverage.

Fitger's also sponsored bowling teams, basketball teams, walkathon pairs, and dance marathon couples. All wore uniforms or, in the case of the dancers, placards,

The Silver Spray dancing bottles pose with other Fitger's employees in front of the brewery.

Annual Spring Sales Meeting

Every spring, Fitger's would bring all its salesmen and distributors to Duluth to acquaint them with new products, forthcoming advertising, pricing, and competition issues. It was a giant pep rally. The three-day session culminated with a banquet and entertainment at one of the hotel ballrooms in Duluth.

The entertainment would include employees or their family members and some other local talent. Sometimes the highlight was a magician or a comedian, but the finale was always a singalong. Some of the people at Fitger's would put new humorous lyrics to a popular tune, chiding the sales people about situations in their territory.

In 1927, the office staff formed a quartet, which sang old and new tunes. Then Elsa Anneke, Victor Anneke's wife, who was a concert pianist, joined with Mrs. Tom Miller, who was a very talented violinist, to perform some classical music. To round out the diversity of entertainment that night, Charlie Zentner—one of the brewery's cellar men—yodeled!

prominently noting their Fitger's Silver Spray sponsorship. There were even dancing bottles of Silver Spray which put on skits of song and comedy in area festivals.

The Fitger Company made a big splash at the Duluth Clinic's grand opening for its new building in 1927. August Fitger's diary noted, "Served Silver Spray Punch made from two hundred bottles of Silver Spray, two hundred oranges, a hundred lemons, and some mint flavor. The patrons liked it very much."

Fitger's continued to participate in parades, a tradition since the Duluth July 4, 1883, parade. Fitger's also sponsored elaborate floats for the big St. Paul Winter Carnival and Minneapolis Aquatennial parades.

Silver Spray Gym is Huge Success

Perhaps the most innovative ideas for promoting Silver Spray came not from the advertising and sales people but from Victor Anneke himself. In September 1927, Anneke opened the Silver Spray Gym at Fitger's. He converted the building that had replaced the old brewery into a boxing gym.

The Silver Spray float took first place in the Duluth Winter Carnival in 1928 and appeared in many community parades.

Boxing was a popular sport at this time, and he hired Jack Hurley, a boxing promoter, to develop a boxing program and encourage youths to participate. Anneke believed the gym would be a benefit to the community and also would create good publicity for Fitger's.

The Silver Spray Gym was a first class facility. The main floor was a boxing arena with a seating capacity of 1,200. The basement was a training facility. Anneke spent $5,000 for equipment and the brewery carpenters built the facilities. There were modern steam rooms, showers, lockers, rubbing tables, mats, and other training equipment. Jack Hurley hired Phil Turk, a trainer, and the Silver Spray Gym rapidly became one of the best gyms in the region. Hurley gained fame for himself and for Silver Spray Gym by handling a boxer from Fargo, North Dakota, named Billy Petrolle. Under Hurley, Petrolle, known as the "Fargo Express," was able to get fights in the Chicago area and in New York at Madison Square Garden.

The gym became a stopping point for people on their way up the boxing career ladder, a training ground for aspiring pugs. The Silver Spray Gym catered the local fights; bigger fights were held in a venue that could hold more people, such as the Curling Club. The Silver Spray Gym sponsored smaller promotions, usually aimed at the youth, in conjunction with the major fights at larger facilities.

Middleweight Angelo "Killer" Puglisi, a popular Duluth boxer who trained at the Silver Spray gym, in a 1930 promotional photo. Puglisi went 19-18-3 with 11 knock outs.

Heavyweight Contender

German heavyweight contender Max Schmeling visited the Silver Spray Gym in the late 1920s. On June 13, 1930, he became the heavyweight champion of the world by defeating Jack Sharkey with a fourth-round foul. Sharkey won the title back from Schmeling on June 21, 1932, in a fifteen-round decision. But on June 19, 1936, Schmeling KO'd the unbeaten Joe Louis in twelve rounds, a big propaganda win for Germany and the Nazis' talk of Aryan superiority.

When Louis, (a.k.a. the "Brown Bomber") won the heavyweight title from James J. Braddock in eight rounds on June 22, 1937, he refused to be called champ until he made up for his only professional loss—he needed to beat Schmeling. Of course, it was more than a personal rivalry. In a White House visit less than a month before the fight, President Roosevelt told Louis "Joe, we need muscles like yours to beat Germany." With all of America behind him and international attention focused on the match, Louis KO'd Schmeling in one round on June 22, 1938, bursting the Nazis' propaganda balloon in a mere 124 seconds. Schmeling never challenged Louis again.

The Silver Spray Bubbles Orchestra

Victor Anneke was always looking for new ways to promote Silver Spray and, for a short time, sponsored an orchestra for dances in smaller communities surrounding Duluth. There were six players in the orchestra and each received $50 a week. The Fitger Company also furnished a coat and tie for each of the musicians. The orchestra had numerous engagements around the area and things were going very well until the latter part of the four-week experiment, when the members of the orchestra were involved in a minor automobile accident.

The man who drove into the dance band had not been following Prohibition laws at the time of the accident. A newspaper reporter could not resist making light of the incident, writing, "The orchestra crashed into discordant music. The drum boomed forth on a hollow note. The violin gave faint squeaks and the muted cornet and the trombones clattered. There was no music for the dance last night at the Lake Nebagamon. The Silver Spray Bubbles Orchestra, more or less punctured, failed to arrive." The publicity, though lighthearted, was not welcomed at Fitger's. After the accident, the Fitger's Silver Spray Bubbles Orchestra disbanded. Fitger's would again hire its own band of local musicians in the late 1930s and early 1940s.

August Fitger Moves On—and Loses His Partner

In 1928, August Fitger moved permanently to Beverly Hills, California. His work at Celite Corporation over the previous five years had resulted in winning an award sponsored by a major shipbuilding firm to develop a better method to insulate boilers. The Celite product significantly outperformed better-known national companies in tests performed by the firm. Winning the competition, however, brought Celite to the attention of the bigger firms, and the Johns-Manville Corporation started an aggressive campaign to convince Fitger to sell to them. Later that year, Fitger agreed to sell Celite Corporation to Johns-Manville for nearly $9 million.

That same year, his brewery partner Percy Anneke, who had never fully recovered from a stroke suffered five years earlier, passed away.

Fitger Sells His Duluth Home

After finally moving to California permanently, the Fitgers no longer needed their large house in Duluth. During their many previous absences, the house had been broken into on a number of occasions and theft occurred.

The house had been completed in 1893 at a cost of nearly $11,000. About ten years later another several thousand dollars was spent on a major remodeling project. But the housing market was slumping in 1928, just one year prior to the stock market crash. Previously, Fitger had refused a $15,000 sale for his home, but in 1928 he was forced to sell for only $10,000—much less than it was worth.

CHAPTER 13

Prohibition Finally Leaves

Silver Spray had spurred Fitger's beverage sales to a 1927 peak of 220 railroad cars delivered nationwide. At this time, however, the business climate throughout the country and even the world started to show signs of slowing. In 1928, Fitger's loaded only 180 railroad cars; by 1931, Fitger's would load a mere 99 cars.

The stock market crash in 1929, following two years of sluggish sales, proved too much for many of the breweries struggling to stay open during Prohibition. The Minneapolis Brewing Company, a coalition of four breweries formed in 1893 and brewer of Grain Belt Beer, closed as a result. Northern Brewery in Superior had lost its license to brew non-intoxicating cereal beverages and been forced to close after government agents founds kegs of illegal, intoxicating beer in one of its employee's vehicles. People's Brewery of Duluth was auctioned under court order for $10,548 in 1931. In 1930, the owner of the Rex Company (formerly Duluth Brewing and Malting Company) sold the business property (not including real estate) of his beverage division, the Sobriety Company, to Fitger's. The Rex Company, which had changed its name when national prohibition went into effect, then closed its doors for business. From that purchase, the Fitger Company received title to

labels such as Minnesota Club Ginger Ale, the Lovit pop line, the Rex and Royal Brew cereal beverages, the Moose label, and other brands, bottles, and equipment.

The purchase from Rex increased production at Fitger's. In addition, Fitger's came out with three new products—a citrus drink called "Lindy Julep," a carbonated water called "Kitchi Gammi," and a ginger ale, another carbonated water, and a lime rickey under the brand name "Isle Royale," which was very popular.

Unfortunately, whatever Fitger's did could not compensate for the losses due to Prohibition. John Beerhalter said, "With the large plant in a high-tax city, the Fitger Company lost money every year during the 1920s."

Desperate Measures

Victor Anneke had recurring heart trouble and other health problems throughout the 1930s. While sick in bed at home in 1931, he contemplated closing the brewery. He had been optimistic that Prohibition would have been repealed long before this time, and despite producing and distributing a wide variety of products and using very creative marketing and promotions, the Fitger Company kept losing money. When Anneke called John

A bottle for Lovit, a line of soda from the Rex Company.

Beerhalter and Walter Johnson to his home to discuss the options, Beerhalter convinced him to keep the brewery open, as he believed the repeal of Prohibition was just around the corner.

Anneke agreed to follow Beerhalter's suggestion only if there were drastic cuts in expenses. Fitger's cut its payroll significantly and only three salesmen remained. In addition to cutting payroll, Fitger's got out of the candy and cigar business and concentrated on selling beverages. All the remaining candy was sold to a local company, Barsness Candy. The cigars were sold to the Rust Parker wholesale house in Duluth. The Fitger Company was doing everything possible to hold on until Prohibition ended.

Anneke brought in his father-in-law, Charles Krause of Saint Louis, to make some of the personnel cuts. Anneke had personal ties with many of the people that had to be laid off, especially Thomas Miller, and found it too to difficult to do himself.

Anneke was committed to doing everything possible to keep the core employees working. Fortunately, signs of improvement for the brewing industry started appearing at the national political level before the end of 1931.

Change on the Horizon

In 1932, Victor Anneke was optimistic that the end of Prohibition was very near and began preparing for that day. The majority of the public was demanding the repeal of Prohibition and this motivated many politicians to take steps to "loosen" Prohibition laws. Brewers were now receiving increased support when they argued that Congress had broad power to redefine "non-intoxicating" without waiting for repeal of the Prohibition Amendment. Congress took the first step in early 1932 when it passed a law allowing breweries to sell wort, the liquid found in the brewing kettle, where hops are added to the malt mash and the mixture is heated. The wort was not considered beer because yeast had not been added and allowed to ferment.

The changing mood of the country became apparent during the 1932 presidential election between Franklin Roosevelt and the incumbent, President Herbert Hoover. Roosevelt advocated the repeal of Prohibition and won the election in a landslide.

Beer Comes Back

Victor Anneke was ill again early in 1933, and was not at the brewery from January through March. He recovered just in time. By the time Roosevelt was inaugurated in March 1933, Congress had been working many months to redefine "non-intoxicating" and quickly presented the new President

with a "Beer Bill." On March 21, 1933, President Roosevelt signed the law allowing states to decide if 3.2 percent alcohol beer was "non-intoxicating," and, therefore, legal.

On April 6, 1933, two weeks after the "Beer Bill" had been signed, it became legal to sell 3.2 beer in those individual states which had passed enabling legislation. Many state legislatures were not in session and hence only nineteen states had laws in effect allowing beer to be sold on April 6. Minnesota was one state that was ready for the return of beer.

Four days after the "Beer Bill" was signed into law, the Minnesota legislature passed a bill making 3.2 beer

Labels from Fitger's and Rex Company's non-alcoholic beverages.

legal in the state. Governor Floyd B. Olson signed the bill into law on March 25, 1933. The Duluth City Council began work immediately and held special sessions to determine the license fees for on- and off-sale beer outlets. The original fee was $300 for an on-sale license and $50 for an off-sale license. The on-sale fee was reduced to $150 when the council learned that Minneapolis was charging only $100 for an on-sale license. The Council also drew demarcation lines for five districts in town where the sale of beer would be legal. In St. Louis County, the fee for an on-sale license was only $50.

Fitger's Gets Ready

In March, Victor had hired John Beerhalter's son, Richard, to open a Fitger's agency for the new 3.2 beer in Superior. In noting the appointment, the newspaper was delighted to report that Richard's telephone number was "32."

The brewery had a lack of storage for case beer because much of the space had been turned over to Silver Spray and other soft drink production. Victor anticipated tremendous sales that first day, so he hired back a full crew and ordered six empty boxcars to be set in place behind the brewery for extra storage for case beer once production began.

Fitger's bottled 3.2 beer under the Natural Beer label, even though it had been used earlier for 4.0 beer only. Because Fitger's had stayed open through Prohibition making near beer (and other beverages), all the machinery was in good operating condition. Near beer was actually made from "real" beer—once "real" beer was made, the product was simply brought back to the brewing kettle where the alcohol was "boiled" out. Fitger's task of retooling for beer production was therefore much easier than at many other breweries that had closed during Prohibition. Wort for the beer had already

Opposite: Charles Zentner, the cellar boss (standing), and Frank Franckowiak test the first batch of 3.2 beer. It would be kegged, bottled, and ready for sale on April 6, 1933.

been made, simplifying the task of actually brewing the beer, and thus allowing time to age the beer properly before the big day. All fermenting and aging tanks were filled to capacity by April 6, 1933.

Roll Out the Barrels

Excitement was brewing throughout the city in the anticipation of 3.2 beer becoming legal, and Hollywood could not have written a better script. Fitger's had been

The return of beer. The beer was 3.2 percent alcohol by weight, but could also be described as the equivalent 4.0 percent alcohol by volume. Using the higher number gave customers the perception that it was stronger beer, and increased sales.

locked up at six in the evening on April 5, 1933, to make sure nobody tried to break in prior to midnight. Empty trucks were lined up two abreast from Fifth Avenue East to Seventh Avenue East. Additional trucks were locked inside the brewery yard awaiting the signal to be loaded.

The beer parade started promptly at midnight. Police Sergeant Elmer Stovern fired a pistol as the starting signal, and Scott Cash, an inspector for the Federal Bureau of Industrial Alcohol, unlocked the gates to the brewery. A German "Oompah" band immediately struck up with the popular song "Happy Days are Here Again."

Inside Fitger's, Victor Anneke hosted a gala party in the boardroom. WEBC radio had its remote broadcasting equipment there for the occasion, and Victor Anneke spoke over the airwaves, enthusiastically welcoming the return of legal beer drinking (see sidebar). Next door at the Pickwick, and at other cafes, hotels, and taverns in and around Duluth, the general public began celebrating during regular business hours later that day.

August Fitger's diary noted that 147 trucks were loaded after midnight. On that first day, April 6, 1933, Fitger's sold 19,000 cases of beer, plus 1,260 kegs of beer.

Victor Anneke Welcomes Back Beer (His radio speech, broadcast on April 6, 1933)

Tonight marks an historic moment in the progress of Duluth and the nation. After fifteen years of enforced idleness, a great industry goes back to work again. Thousands of men are being put on new payrolls. Millions of dollars are being spent in this renewed activity. Tonight, as I said, is historic in our national life, for tonight marks more than the legalization of beer. The great principle of government is involved.

Tonight marks the end of the stranglehold which the foes of true temperance have long had upon our laws, and which they have sought, by every means, to enforce upon an unwilling public. Tonight should be remembered, it seems to me, because it was tonight that the right to true temperance, moderation, and good fellowship has been reborn in this country of ours, and the uncontrolled, intemperate drinking of harmful concoctions behind closed doors has been struck a death blow. Good fellowship belongs in the home, the club, or the legitimate hotel and cafe. Let's put it there once more and keep it there.

Good fellowship expresses all our activities here tonight, because we have been able to give employment to men who have long known what it is to hopelessly tramp the streets looking for work. I am more than happy to say, as a citizen of Duluth, that our payroll here at the Fitger plant is now larger than it ever has been in the fifty-two years of our history. The return of beer has permitted us to give honest work to the heads of many Duluth families. Our hotels, our cafes, our grocery stores are now enabled to earn an honest profit on an honest business.

Our facilities for brewing the same old beer have remained with us. Our men, some of whom have been here for forty years, are still on the job and each member of the Fitger organization has been working for months to make your first bottle of Fitger's Beer in 1933 even finer than the last bottle of 1918. The trucks you heard go out of here tonight did not carry green beer. It was fully aged, as fine as any Fitger's ever brewed. The Fitger Company wishes to take this opportunity to pledge to the people of Duluth and the Northwest its word that we shall continue to stand for the finest in beer, as we have for more than half a century.

And now, in closing, before we all go home tonight, let me again say how happy The Fitger Company is at being able to continue its traditions in the great art of brewing appetizing, wholesome beer, and how happy we are to go back to work and to be able to offer employment to so many men.

— Victor Anneke, April 6, 1933

Fitger claimed that in one night, the Federal government "collected $80,000 in excise taxes from Fitger's!" The $80,000 was an exaggeration. It was closer to $8,000, which was still a substantial amount.

Because of the production of beer, employment increased for other businesses as well. A local box factory hired thirty additional men for the making of beer cases. The Duluth Linen Supply Company received large orders for aprons used by barkeeps and beer production crews and hired extra people to fill these orders. The positive effects rippled through the entire United States creating much-needed jobs in a depressed economy.

There was fierce competition among the cafes and taverns in Duluth for their share of the beer market. Many of the cafes started selling eight-ounce glasses of beer for a nickel, which was really only six ounces of

Below: The first truck loaded after the return of beer was headed for Two Harbors. Tim Belland, Fitger's distributor in Two Harbors, is leaning on the side of the truck in the lower left-hand corner.

beer because the head the bartenders put on every glass took up about a quarter of the space. Eventually a beer war began in Duluth and cafes and saloons began selling twelve ounce glasses of beer for a nickel to remain competitive.

Fitger's came out with two new labels for its beer in 1933. Both labels retained the characteristic red star with the sketch of the S.S. *Duluth* in the center. The first version was a green label which dropped the word "Natural." The label had a very brief life; many people associated the color green with beer that wasn't aged properly, using the term "green beer" to describe such an unripened brew. The replacement was just a slight variation of the label Fitger's used for the soft drinks it produced during Prohibition, but brought back "Natural," previously used only on strong, pre-Prohibition beer.

Prohibition Is Repealed

In order for strong beer, wine, and liquor to be sold, the Eighteenth Amendment—the Prohibition Amendment—had to be repealed. Congress had started the process for repeal even before passing the "Beer Bill." On February 20, 1933, Congress had proposed the Twenty-first Amendment—the Repeal Amendment. Three-fourths of the individual states needed to ratify the Repeal Amendment before it could go into effect. A key provision of the Repeal Amendment that led to quick ratification provided that individual states wishing to remain "dry" would get federal assistance for enforcement of state prohibition laws. The Repeal Amendment also required many changes in the way breweries and liquor establishments conducted business. In Minnesota, the Liquor Control Commission established a code of laws that imposed new restrictions on distilleries, wineries, and breweries. For example, breweries could no longer own tied houses. It was also mandatory that the Fitger Company change its name back to "Fitger Brewing Company."

Ratification came on December 5, 1933, legally ending Prohibition.

Looking Back on the Noble Experiment

In 1938, John Beerhalter looked back at Prohibition, which was often referred to as the "Noble Experiment:"

Our nation was just beginning to outgrow its adolescent period when [World War I] and Prohibition came upon us. During the thirteen years our industry was outlawed, we saw crime increase, bootlegging and racketeers gain enormous power, the breakdown of law enforcement, and growth of illegal, inferior products. When the 3.2 beer law passed in 1933, the activities created by our industry took up seven percent of the labor force. Since re-legalization, we have paid about $300 million in brewery wages and salaries and an equal amount for American farm products used in brewing. Breweries are major consumers of grains, especially barley. It takes a whole acre of barley to make 21 barrels of beer. During the past five years, brewers have spent nearly $100 million for wooden and steel barrels and glass bottles and beer cans. We've spent more than $1.5 billion in state and local taxes. And we've spent billions on trucks and machinery, printing and advertising in newspapers and on radio.

In essence, the Noble Experiment did not reduce crime nor help the economy, as its shortsighted proponents believed it would. In fact, it was the reason many of the gangsters, such as Al Capone, gained power and could also have been one of many reasons for the economic downturn known as the recession.

— John Beerhalter

PART IV

Beginnings and Endings

Fitger's Brewery in the 1930s.

CHAPTER 14

The August Fitger Era Ends

Victor Anneke had returned to work just in time to organize the return of 3.2 beer, but was hospitalized during the summer of 1933. On the way back from Big Sandy Lake to Duluth, he and his wife, son, and chauffeur were seriously injured in an automobile accident in Iverson, right outside Cloquet. Victor and his wife, Elsa, spent some time in the Raiter Hospital in Cloquet and then in St. Luke's Hospital in Duluth. Anneke wouldn't return to Fitger's until May of 1934, after missing nearly a year of work. During his absence, Anneke's father-in-law, Charles Krause, managed the brewery.

As fate would have it, August Fitger died the same summer as Anneke's accident. He had lived long enough to see the return of 3.2 beer, but died before the repeal of Prohibition that December.

Fitger had written to John Beerhalter back in September 1932, telling him it was difficult to write a letter, but that "for two old friends, it's an obligation of course." Fitger had also talked about Prohibition. "The most glaring example of fanaticism in our period was the Iowa law which forbade the selling of our product not because it contained alcohol, for it contained none, but because it was made out of barley or barley malt. What a

farce that all was." He had gone on to explain his health. "I wish that I could report more improvement in Mrs. Fitger's and my condition. We both are still fortunate in not suffering any particular pain, except some occasional lumbago myself. About once a week we have even walked about two hundred steps to the dining room, but on the arm of some waiter or our chauffeur. Even writing with a pencil for letters like this one takes five or six times as long as it should. P.S. Dear John, Please send me a photograph of yourself someday."

August Fitger was a multi-talented individual with true German discipline. He began business during the time ice was harvested from Lake Superior and horses and wagons made beer deliveries over dirt roads. At the end of his career, air conditioning units cooled the beer cellars, and insulated railroad cars delivered Fitger's Beer across the region. He was very proud of the fact he was a master brewer who owned his own brewery.

Many other breweries in the area were owned by men who had to hire master brewers or ran their breweries with just practical brewers. Hamm's founder, Theo Hamm, originally was a meat cutter. Joseph Schlitz, a bookkeeper, married the widow of the owner of Krug Brewery and then renamed it for himself. Adolphus Busch, a brewery equipment salesman, married an Anheuser daughter and renamed the E. Anheuser & Company Brewery Association the Anheuser-Busch Brewery Association. Frederick Miller of Miller's Brewery was a German entrepreneur with no brewing experience. Fred Pabst, who preferred to be called "Captain" Pabst because he was a Great Lakes ship captain, married into the Best Brewery family and also renamed the brewery after himself. Jacob Schmidt was a practical brewer whose daughter married a Bremer from a banking family in St. Paul, which assured financing, allowing Schmidt Brewery to continue in business for many years.

Fitger came to Duluth in 1882 to brew beer as Michael Fink's first brew master. Six months later he was a fifty percent partner in Fink's Lake Superior Brewery. In 1885, his friend from Milwaukee, Percy Anneke, bought out Fink's interest and the brewery became A. Fitger & Company Lake Superior Brewery. August Fitger probably never imagined that his name and brewery would be a legacy more than a century after he arrived in Duluth.

Beer in Bottles—and Cans

From 1933 to 1936, Fitger's experienced tremendous growth and record sales. Much of the success was due to the company's continual creation of new products and innovative ways to market them.

Picnic Beer was introduced in 1934, each large bottle containing a half-gallon of non-pasteurized beer—draft

Left: August Fitger in 1907 at age 52. Right: Clara Kirst Fitger was married to August Fitger for forty-eight years, until his death.

beer in a bottle. The product was designed for picnics or other gatherings that were too small to justify buying a keg. Picnic bottles were returnable and reused, but because of the demand for Picnic Beer, an additional 500 cases of Picnic bottles had to be purchased. A sixty-four ounce bottle of Picnic Beer cost forty-nine cents. By comparison, six twelve-ounce bottles of pasteurized beer, totaling seventy-two ounces, sold for forty-five cents.

One of the most successful innovations in the brewing industry was canned beer, and Fitger's became one of the very first companies in the nation and the first brewery in the Midwest to offer canned beer. Tim Belland, the Two Harbors distributor for Fitger's Beer, had gone on a trip to the east coast and noticed some small breweries selling beer in cans. He thought this was a novel idea with great potential and urged Victor Anneke to begin produc-

ing beer in cans. Anneke agreed, and Belland placed the first order of 150 cases of Fitger's Beer in cans. Belland was allowed to take the first delivery of beer in cans to his Two Harbors customers. On November 12, 1935, the first canned beer in the city of Duluth went to the Pickwick—only five cases!

Other new products included the "steinie" which was a short stubby bottle. It had brief success on the market and was discontinued, but reappeared many years later. Fitger's also introduced a new tonic water called Scot Soda, which also did not last long, and a variety of soda flavors under the Arrowhead label. During this time, Fitger's switched from wooden to steel barrels. Even though the

Below: Fitger's first beer can had a cone-shaped top. Right: a bottle of Fitger's Picnic Beer. A can of beer cost more than a bottle of beer, although they both held twelve ounces.

cost of a steel barrel at $7.35 was more than a wooden bar-rel, it eliminated the need for a cooper to repair the wood-en kegs, thus saving money. (Eventually, the brewery switched to lighter-weight aluminum kegs after World War II. Wooden kegs in good repair continued to be used at the brewery on a limited basis until 1948 when Fitger's sold the last remaining wooden kegs, ending an era.)

There was also a new label for Fitger's in this time period; the short-lived green label was replaced with their traditional label with the gold background. Fitger's now used the "Natural Beer" label for both a 3.2 version—for grocery stores and saloons that had only a 3.2 license—and for the revived regular beer, which was differentiated with bold red letters on the label reading "Strong Beer."

Fitger's continued to produce new products. Bock Beer was introduced in 1934, followed by Bock Picnic Beer and Holiday Beer in 1935, which began a tradition of special occasion beers.

Beer Pushes Soda Pop Aside

After Prohibition's repeal, Fitger's focused all its attention on beer. The company essentially abandoned Silver Spray, but did not sell the name or formula. Fitger's produced Silver spray for the local market for about ten more years and thereafter brewed at least one batch of Silver Spray a year to protect their copyright until the mid-1960s.

In 1934, the Silver Spray Gym was dismantled and the area was used for storage and advertising, as it had been in the past. Even so, Fitger's continued to need more room in the existing buildings to accommodate the ever-increasing beer business. Remodeling began on the three-story stable and garage building, built in 1911. Fitger's converted the stable (the last horse had been sold in 1932), which was on the level below Michigan Street, into a garage.

The existing garage on the Michigan Street level was then converted to the Pop Shop, where all soft drinks would be made and bottled, including Silver Spray, Lovit

In the bottle house with Picnic Beer after the end of Prohibition allowed Fitger's to once again make beer.

Life After Silver Spray

After the Silver Spray Gym closed, Phil Turk, the trainer, and Jack Hurley, the manager, left Fitger's and opened a pool hall in Duluth called "The Ringside," where they sold food and beverages. The Ringside was sold a couple years later and, with the help of Fitger's, Turk opened up an establishment on Superior Street called the Smoke Shop, later the Paul Bunyan, which became a popular Duluth bar.

soda pop, Fitger's mixes, and later Squirt. Fitger's purchased the regional franchise for national-brand Squirt in the 1930s. The kettle Beerhalter had bought in Indiana during Silver Spray's heyday was moved into the new space (and would be used until May 1956). Fitger's soft drink operation had been located in the bottle house, the total capacity of which was now available for beer. The top floor of the garage continued to be used as the carpenter's shop. The Fitger's carpenters and tinners did all the remodeling work on the lower two floors.

Owners and Employees Benefit from Record Sales

In 1936, employment was at full strength. A new union contract had to be negotiated, in which Fitger's agreed to the demand from the International Union of Brewery Workers for a five percent increase in wages, which was considered substantial in those days. Group life insurance was included in the benefit package. Fitger's underwrote a recreation club, which, among other events, sponsored the Fitger picnics from then on. The company also made loans available to employees at reasonable interest rates. This loan program evolved into the establishment of the Fitger's Credit Union a few years later.

It was amazing that Fitger's sales were very strong while many businesses were struggling or had closed. Money was in short supply and in April 1936, Fitger's

borrowed $90,000 to be used for improvements to the brewery. They were able to repay all the principal and interest by the end of the year. In the present day, this figure would be close to $2 million, which would be a substantial obligation for any small business, especially during a time like the Depression.

Fitger's continued to set new sales records. By 1936, Fitger's shipped a record-setting 417 carloads of beer and also set a single-day sales record of 818 barrels. This allowed its board of directors to declare a five-percent dividend for the year.

The Tap Room

Fitger's had leased the Pickwick at Prohibition's start, leaving Fitger's without a traditional in-house saloon upon the return of beer. When Prohibition was repealed, the

The return of the Natural Beer label, in its 3.2 version.

bottom level of the office building (one floor below the current lobby of Fitger's Inn) was therefore converted into the "Tap Room." It was fairly modest in décor when compared to bars at other breweries (and the old mural-filled Brewery Saloons in Fitger's past). The tables were plain and it had a piano, pool table, and a fireplace. New beer tokens were made, the same shape but slightly larger than pre-Prohibition tokens. (Tokens during World War II would be made of cardboard or wood because of the scarcity of metals.)

The Tap Room also was used for sales meetings, employee holiday parties, recreation club meetings, and as a meeting place for the summer tours. (Following World War II, many returning veterans would hold their stag parties at the Tap Room.) The brewery also rented out the facilities, including the bartender and an unlimited supply of beer, for $10 a night. This fee lasted into the 1960s. The room had chairs for forty to fifty people, but on many occasions, up to eighty would be in the Tap Room at one time.

A post-Prohibition beer token, front and back, good for one free beer at the new Tap Room.

Labels from Fitger's post-Prohibition Beers

Fitger's Bock Picnic Beer (below) advertised as "GENUINE KEG BEER," Bock Beer (at right, with traditional goat's head signifying a bock beer), and Fitger's Holiday Beer (lower right).

CHAPTER 15

From Son to Son

Victor Anneke's health continued to deteriorate and his father-in-law, Charles Krause, was spending more and more time in Duluth to help with brewery matters while Anneke was at a rehabilitation spa in Mineral Wells, Texas. Krause was getting up in years and felt that Anneke needed a more permanent solution for management assistance.

Arnold Fitger and Victor Anneke had remained friends since their childhood. Fitger was in charge of many successful companies in California and did not visit Duluth frequently, but he did keep in touch with Anneke and they consulted often. Fitger was elected to the board of directors of the brewery in 1936, and within a few months, Anneke asked Fitger to take over the management responsibilities.

Anneke delegated other responsibilities as well. Writing from Mineral Wells to Beerhalter on February 20, 1937, Anneke gave Beerhalter the green light to do what he thought best for brewery operations: "I would be so much more satisfied with the new machinery and the remodeling of the cooling room. You don't have to tell me how much money you are spending. And from now on, I imagine you will have to go full speed ahead."

Anneke knew that changes were coming now that Fitger was going to manage the brewery. Fitger first visited the brewery as manager in February 1937 and stayed for eight days. He made a swift appraisal of the situation and made changes immediately. He informed Anneke by letter:

"When you get in Duluth, you will find that I have made some changes in the office. If I'm going to operate the Fitger Brewing Company by remote control, as I must do, I can only do it if I have a very close cooperation among the men that are doing the actual work in Duluth. In order to do this, I have asked John [Beerhalter] and Walter [Johnson] to move their desks into the back office, which is the Board Room. John and Walter will sit side by side and I've asked John to pass on all the work done by Walter as well as by Lou Dillon, the sales manager. Mr. Dillon is in the same office Mr. Thompson used. This puts the three important men right close to each other. If I were in Duluth, I might not want to operate just that way, but in as much as I cannot be there all this time, I will have to get these men this close together so that they will have to function together."

Fitger's letter also went on to tell how other employees in the office were placed. This was just the beginning of his writing, which usually amounted to two or three letters a day. In order to maintain close contact while running the brewery from Los Angeles, Fitger wrote daily to Beerhalter, the superintendent and master brewer; Johnson, the secretary treasurer; and accountant Hilbert "Bert" Jeronimus.

Simply yours Jimmie and Jackie #8 Pike Lake Walkathon Duluth, Minn.

Photo Goddard

In a response to Fitger, dated May 5, 1937, Anneke, who was still in Texas at the spa, wrote: "Mr. Krause was indeed happy to meet you and spoke of the dynamic fortitude you displayed in getting around the country. He complimented me on picking the very best man available. I am passing this on to you for stepping up and taking such excellent hold of the reins and relieving me of all the responsibility.

"...An additional entertainment here this week. The undertakers of Oklahoma and Texas are holding their convention. These health resorts think of the greatest modes of entertainment. The one lobby is full of caskets, vaults, burial clothing, embalming apparatus and everything else that goes with the dead. The sidewalks and streets are lined with ambulances, dead wagons and hearses and so forth. We have been invited today to witness a vivisection of a corpse, but we declined. Have said enough."

A New Advertising Campaign

Even though Fitger's had penetrated the national market with Silver Spray soda, beer was sold only in the immediate region. Fitger had hired Louis Dillon as sales manager to expand into the Minneapolis market. Dillon's salary was second only to Arnold Fitger himself. Fitger's then opened a distribution

Jackie and Jimmie, a Fitger's-sponsored team at the Pike Lake Walkathon.

center in the Twin Cities to serve seven new southern Minnesota distributors, and Dillon hired a salesman to oversee the accounts in the area. Arnold Fitger also hired a new advertising agency, the Burnett Agency out of Chicago, for both the new distribution area and the existing Fitger's territories. Fitger's always prided itself on its advertising and marketing programs. The overall concept was to bring attention to their products while focusing on fun; for instance, Fitger's sponsored many sporting teams and was very involved in the community.

Leo Burnett, the head of the advertising agency (who later became internationally recognized in the book *A Hundred Men and Women Who Made the Last One Hundred Years Great*), decided on a sportsmen theme. He used fish-

A newspaper ad touting Fitger's Natural Beer as the "he-man's beer."

Arnold Fitger Comes to Duluth

In August 1937, Fitger rented a place at Schultz Lake for his family, had telephone service installed, and had Walker Jamar make a rowboat for use on the lake. Fitger borrowed a trailer from Richard Beerhalter, John's son, to transport the boat. He also sent his own automobile, a Pierce Arrow, on a flatbed car from California. His wife needed a car too, so Fitger had a Chrysler Airflow shipped by boat from the factory in Detroit to Duluth to be waiting for her upon their arrival. When Beerhalter got information that the Pierce Arrow had arrived, he sent an employee to retrieve the automobile, drive it to the brewery, and wash it. The same was done when the Chrysler Airflow arrived. Everyone helped to make Fitger's move to Duluth enjoyable. When the Fitgers returned to Schultz Lake the following August, brewery employees even stocked the lake with fish as a good luck charm for Fitger.

ing and hunting pictures in the campaign, a change from current advertising and thus expensive for Fitger's. Ground work for the campaign started in the spring of 1937 with several meetings between the Fitger hierarchy and the Burnett Agency. The campaign kicked off that August, concentrating on Fitger's Natural Beer, referring to it as the he-man's beer—the way beer had tasted prior to Prohibition.

The new campaign featured a radio program, newspaper ads, posters, billboards, and new point-of-sale pieces. All forms of advertising in the summer featured the fishing contest. Fitger's gave away South Bend tackle outfits every week for sixteen weeks to the fishermen with the biggest fish in four categories—muskie, walleyed pike, bass, and northern pike. The first year of the contest, 8,941 pounds of fish were entered from Minnesota, Wisconsin, the Dakotas, Iowa, Illinois, and Missouri.

The weekly winners were announced on the "Fitger's Sportsman's Special" radio program that was broadcast every Friday night in front of a live audience at WCCO Radio in Minneapolis and also carried on WEBC in Duluth, WHLB in Virginia, and WMFG in Hibbing. Clelland Card was the emcee. The WCCO radio audience covered all of southern Minnesota, northern Iowa, and western Wisconsin and was a major factor in developing Fitger's name recognition in the new markets. Besides promoting the fishing contest, the program also featured fishing tips, skits, and lots of music from the WCCO chorus and orchestra and from other area musicians. When "The Fitger's Sportsman's Special" came to Duluth for a production at the Duluth Armory, three thousand people showed up for the live program.

And a New Beer

August 1937 was a busy month for Fitger's. In addition to the radio show and fishing contest featuring Fitger's Natural Beer, Fitger's also introduced a new beer (with a different label) called "Nordlager," which had its own ad campaign. Nordlager was designed for the 3.2 outlets and was introduced as a price point beer. It sold for ten cents a bottle compared to fifteen cents for Fitger's premium Natural Beer. An airplane was commissioned to write in the sky, "Call Melrose 1280," the Fitger's Brewery phone number. The authorized promotion had been kept under wraps without the knowledge of most brewery officials. The phones rang off the hook and for the next two days the airplane wrote in the sky, "Buy Nordlager."

The ad campaign featured various themes: "Brewed for the North Country;" "Nordlager has character, tang, zest and pep;" "Full of Minnesota's sunshine;" and "Packed with the Northland's golden grain goodness."

The Nordlager introductory ad concluded, "Made right, aged right, flavored right. Because it's made by that master brewer of Fitger's, John Beerhalter, foremost of brewmasters in the whole Northwest. Try Fitger's Nordlager—and make a new beer friend for life." There followed, as usual, another mention of the fishing contest and radio show.

The brewery also printed a small newspaper called "Fitger's Nordlager News," which listed the names of the winners of the fishing contests and the fishing equipment they won. In the fall, Fitger's started a new promotion that

awarded a pedigree hunting dog for the person who mailed in the best name for the dog. Some of the dogs were featured at Fitger's booth at the Minnesota State Fair.

Victor Anneke Dies

In August 1937, after several months in Texas, Victor Anneke had also returned to Duluth, but was almost immediately admitted to the hospital for a heart ailment,

Carpenters and Tinners

All the construction work required at Fitger's was done by a very gifted group of carpenters and tinners. Joseph Ario, a carriage maker from a part of Austria that is now Poland, joined Fitger's as a carpenter and cabinetmaker in the early 1900s and was the foreman of the carpenter shop until it closed in 1942. Prior to joining Fitger's, he had helped build the cribbing of Duluth's first ship canal and also Elevator A, Duluth's first grain elevator. Carpenters over the years included Joe Der, Pete Wolowicz, Carl Leland, and Joseph Ario's son, Dick.

The carpenters and tinners were responsible for interior construction projects and made furniture for the brewery, tied houses, and the Fitger and Anneke real estate properties and homes. Leo Glopa and Louie Surman, who were tinners, worked with the carpenters on many projects. The tinners fashioned the inner linings for tavern coolers, spigots, and decorative metalwork for the bars and back bars. At first they used what is called German silver, an alloy of copper, zinc, and nickel. Glopa and Surman then developed a method for welding stainless steel and began using this stronger material for the liners.

The carpenters built the original ornate bars and back bars for the Brewery Saloon, now the Pickwick, and many other saloons across the Fitger territory. The upper part of the original back bar they made for the old Brewery Saloon in 1894, which was moved to the new Brewery Saloon in 1915, is still used at the Pickwick today. The hand-made cold chests in the back bar have been replaced by commercial versions, but most of the wall-mounted fixtures have been preserved. Joseph Ario also traveled throughout Fitger's territory to build, repair, or tear down ice houses near northern Minnesota lakes where ice was harvested for Fitger's distributors in those areas. On one such trip, Ario took the train from Duluth to Hibbing and then traveled to International Falls by dogsled. After refrigeration became available, Ario no longer needed to travel.

Ario's daughter, Marion, recalled that due to cold winds blowing off Lake Superior, the shop was so cold that her father wore long johns even in the summer. The windows were kept open for fresh air because of all the sawdust in the shop. Only the finishing area was closed, to keep the dust out. Marion Ario also remembered that the Fitger's carpenters had their own method of recycling in those days. "Anything that was torn down or replaced could be used any way my dad chose," she explained. "At my home we had a mantel and several doors from the Fitger or Anneke homes. I rescued a small, damaged gate leg table my father used as a stand for paint cans. Father repaired it and refinished it and it now stands by my bed today. My two oak dressers are made from old cabinets that were taken out of some tavern. My dining room chairs are made from the oak of a dismantled aging barrel. I have a Japanese bowl that my dad found hidden in one of the ice houses he tore down."

among other issues. When he was finally able to go home, he fell down the stairs and broke an arm. Beerhalter wrote, "He broke his right arm close to the shoulder. The doctors were unable to put it in a cast, keeping some tension on with weights. This morning (October 14) they reported his heart was acting up. He was in an oxygen tent."

Victor Anneke managed to go to the office one last time for a few hours that week, but passed away at St. Mary's Hospital on October 20, 1937. Long-time Fitger's employees had nothing but praise for him. They remembered him as a sportsman and snappy dresser, "like the Crown Prince," one employee said. Duluthians in general remembered him for his civic involvement and generosity.

The Fitgers Purchase Anneke Shares

When Victor Anneke died, some local Duluth businessmen approached John Beerhalter to report that a consortium of people were interested in purchasing the brewery. Beerhalter immediately relayed this information to Arnold Fitger, who replied that he was thankful that some people in Duluth were interested, but that he anticipated buying the brewery himself. The Anneke estate owned sixty-nine percent of Fitger's common stock, and the Fitger family owned twenty-three percent. Beerhalter and P.C. Schmidt, the Fitger's attorney, each had 105 shares. Walter Johnson and Anneke's father-in-law, Charles Krause, each had 100 shares.

Arnold Fitger was very busy in California with his varied interests. The additional burden of a brewery seemed over-taxing, but it was the brewery that had given the Fitgers the impetus to branch out into other ventures.

Arnold felt an obligation to keep the brewery and its name afloat. Besides, he had a financial interest in it.

By the spring of 1938, Arnold Fitger and the Fitger family had purchased the Anneke family shares in the brewery. However, Fitger still spent a great deal of time in California tending to his other businesses. He had started a company called Kelco, which developed products using kelp, and was president of the Refactories Corporation, the Fitger California Company, and the Horseshoe Cattle Company. He was also general manager of the Metalite Corporation in California.

Fitger had developed a heart problem and taking care of all the businesses was becoming difficult. Every day he had to correspond with the brewery from California, sometimes writing fourteen to fifteen pages per day, often dictating to a stenographer. When he was at his ranch, letters were forwarded from the Los Angeles office, and he called back to Los Angeles to dictate his replies. Even though Fitger was not present at Fitger's on a day-to-day basis, he managed the operation very efficiently. He gave stock as an incentive to key office personnel. He also named John Beerhalter, whom he believed was the most qualified person, as president of the Fitger Brewing Company. This ended fifty-seven continuous years of the Fitger and Anneke families' direct management of the brewery. Richard Kohtz, who had started as August Fitger's chauffeur in 1918, and had remained working in the bottle house when August moved to California in 1928, now became superintendent. Arnold remained chairman of the board, and his family still had controlling interest of Fitger's stock.

CHAPTER 16

Before and After the War

When Arnold Fitger had taken over the brewery, the company was rich in real estate. During 1938 and 1939, business around the country was still stagnant and money was in short supply. Therefore, Fitger's sold some buildings, originally purchased to become tied houses, for approximately $60,000 to buy much needed equipment including a pasteurizer, a bottling machine capable of bottling two hundred bottles per minute, a washer, and a soaker. One parcel sold became, for a time, the site of the Duluth Chamber of Commerce. Three other parcels in Virginia also were sold, including the Dowling and Pigott buildings. There was a proposal to sell the Pickwick property, but Fitger felt that this was much too close to the brewery to sell.

In his letters to Beerhalter, Fitger passed on recommendations handed down by his father. For example, he told Beerhalter that after a day's work, his father would call on a special account or two just to see how things were going, and he recommended this to Beerhalter. Fitger didn't hesitate to inform Beerhalter of his importance to the Fitger Brewing Company. So when Beerhalter wanted to go deer or duck hunting he had the ability to do so. Many of the

Left: Removing the old washer. Right: Yardmen prepare to unload one part of the new soaker machine with a small crane.

Above: Bottle house machinery in the late 1940s.

Below: Fitger's Rex "Imperial Dry" Beer.

advertising calendars used in the 1940s showed pictures of Beerhalter and friends enjoying the great outdoors.

New Beers and New Marketing

In 1939, Fitger's came out with Fitger's Premium Pale Beer. The beer was not well received and was discontinued in March 1941. Meanwhile, Fitger's Natural Beer was sidelined and a label emphasizing "Fitger Endorsed" was created; this label was also short lived. After this, Fitger's promoted Rex, which had been used occasionally as both a strong beer and a Picnic Beer after Fitger's purchased the name from the Duluth Brewing and Malting Company in 1930. Rex was reintroduced in 1939–1940 with the new slogan, "Naturally Brewed—Naturally Better," which was one of Fitger's best and probably longest-lived advertising themes; advertising Fitger's as a natural beer had started in the early 1900s. Rex became very popular and Fitger's continued to produce it until the early 1960s.

Nordlager, a big hit since its inception in 1937, continued to be a featured beer in 1939. The 1939 ad cam-

Label for the short-lived Premium Pale Beer.

paign concentrated on Nordlager with a media blitz that tied in radio, newspaper, point of sale, and continued fishing contest advertising. There were two new advertising themes: "Brewed the Honest Way" and "The Fitger Folks." Pictures of key brewery people were highlighted in newspaper ads and Fitger's calendars. The 1930s brought prosperity and dynamic changes to Fitger's, which had started the decade as one of the few breweries across the nation still operating during Prohibition. By 1939, a brewery directory showed twenty-three breweries operating in Minnesota, three of them in Duluth, down from more than seventy Minnesota breweries before Prohibition.

Below: May 23, 1939, ad in the Duluth Herald. *Top right: Certificate and card for winners of 1939 fishing contest.*

FREE! $2250.00 worth of PRIZES
TO FISHERMEN WHO LIKE BEER!

64 beautiful South Bend Tackle Outfits, and 320 cases of Fitger's Nordlager Beer, go FREE to lucky fishermen

Arnold Fitger Dies

In 1942, Arnold Fitger died in California at the age of 51. He was a veteran of World War I and took an active part in the American Legion Post in Beverly Hills. He was a member of the California Club and the Los Angeles and Bel Air Country Clubs. A Los Angeles newspaper that reported his death in its general news columns called

In line for their fishing licenses are, from left to right, Arnold Fitger, John Beerhalter Jr., and John Beerhalter Sr. At far right is Walter Johnson, a longtime Fitger's employee.

him an industrialist and noted that Fitger was president of his four California-based companies.

Arnold Fitger was considered a very talented businessman. He knew how to scrutinize balance sheets, but at the same time he was very compassionate to his employees in all the businesses he managed. He had purchased the Kelco Company just one month before the stock market crash of 1929 and times had been difficult, but he made one objective clear in a letter in the 1930s: "My greatest pride lies in the number of years that so many of our men have been with us. We just must not permit anything to happen to our company that will cause the old men to lose their jobs...."

After Fitger's death, the Fitger estate continued ownership and control of Fitger's Brewery. Many people believed that the stress of his many responsibilities had contributed to his early death. The employees at all the companies he had managed missed Arnold Fitger.

The Fitger family place of rest in Forest Home Cemetery, Milwaukee, Wisconsin. The graves of other brewing moguls are found there as well, including Blatz, Pabst, and Schlitz..

The War Years

During World War II, it became increasingly difficult to get many of the resources that the brewery needed, such as malt, cans, bottles, and bottle caps, because agricultural products, raw materials, and manufacturing capacity were diverted to the war effort. If new items could not be found, Fitger's would clean up and reuse items, such as old bottle caps. Everything was recycled during this time of continued shortages. This was similar to what had happened during World War I, so the company brewed War Beer once again. War Beer used fewer ingredients but still met the alcoholic content standards of both strong and 3.2 beer. It was considered a "watered-down" beer. Workers were also in short supply, so Fitger's hired women to work in the bottle house. In the other brewing operations, however, only trained,

From left to right, Arnold Fitger, John Beerhalter Sr., Walter Johnson, and Fred Hitchcock, Fitger's sales manager.

A Family Tradition

Just as Arnold Fitger and Victor Anneke had eventually worked at Fitger's Brewery, so did John Beerhalter Sr.'s sons. In addition to John Beerhalter Jr., Richard Beerhalter was sales manager and Erwin Beerhalter managed the Pop Shop.

Not every relative worked in management. Herb Callies, a nephew of John Beerhalter Sr., was employed as a full-time painter. Every spring, he would start at one end of the brewery, painting window trim, doors, and any other painted surface on the exterior of the brewery. In the winter he would paint the interior. When spring rolled around again, he would start on the exterior at the point where he stopped the previous fall. Once he finished the entire complex of buildings, he would go back to where he had begun painting and start the entire process all over again.

experienced men were employed, many of them too old for the draft. In 1942, the carpenters shop was closed because of material shortages and Joseph Ario, the foreman, retired at age seventy-two (see sidebar, page 107). Otherwise, business was strong at the brewery and the best-selling beer in the region was Fitger's Rex.

In January 1944, John Beerhalter Sr. had a massive stroke that forced him to learn to walk and talk again. He offered to resign but the Fitger family refused to accept his resignation. He returned to work in May 1944, but could no longer put in the long hours he had in the past. The elder Beerhalter would come to work around nine in the morning and park his new Buick in front of the office. The brewery mechanic would help him out of the car and get him into the office. Beerhalter would leave in the afternoon at an earlier-than-normal time. John Beerhalter Sr. remained president but relinquished his brewmaster duties to his son John Beerhalter Jr.

"Rosie the Bottler"—women were a big part of the bottle house crew during World War II.

Post-War Changes

Fitger's began brewing regular beer again, now that materials were available. The phrase "Imperial Dry Beer" was added to the Rex label at this time. After the War, many companies retooled for what they believed would be an economic expansion, and Fitger's installed new, modern equipment throughout the brewery. The company purchased full-page newspaper ads that featured the new equipment and stated that Fitger's beer was made from "Pure Lake Superior Water." The ads also featured formal portraits of John Beerhalter Sr. and John Beerhalter Jr.

The full-page ad pictured five new pieces of machinery, stating that the beer was more pure due to the new equipment. Aging tanks were all made of redwood, with no nails used in their construction. The new finishing tanks were constructed of steel and lined with glass. The old finishing tanks had been made of oak. All wooden vessels were coated with beer varnish so the beer never touched the wood. Another part of the ad was a personal discourse on beer making by John Beerhalter Sr.

From Father to Son, Again

In 1948, John Beerhalter Sr. became chairman of the board and his son John Beerhalter Jr. became president. Walter Johnson remained vice-president and treasurer, and Bert Jeronimus was secretary and assistant treasurer.

Top: A Fitger's Rex beer token (front and back).

Above: Post–World War II Rex label.

Following page: Fitger's ad featured in a newspaper's special annual industrial section.

Troubles with Clear Bottles

By the late 1940s, Fitger's used only dark brown bottles for beer because Beerhalter felt beer in clear bottles went "skunky" too quickly, especially when out in the sunshine. In 1948, the old four-story wooden ice house contained nearly twenty thousand beer cases with half-a-million empty bottles in them. Fitger's sold all its clear bottles to Duluth Brewing and Malting. Each day, anyone who was available would go into the old ice house, find the cases with clear bottles, and load them onto a box car that delivered the bottles to Duluth Brewing and Malting.

That brewery used the clear bottles for a beer called "Royal Bohemian." Then it brewed another beer in a clear bottle called "Royal 57," so named because its alcoholic content by volume was 5.7 percent. When the Heinz 57 Company sued the company for using the number "57," Duluth Brewing and Malting changed Royal 57 to Royal 58.

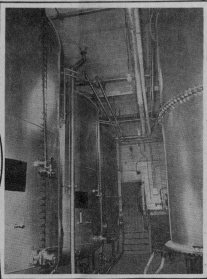

CHAPTER 17

The Beginning of the End

In 1951, Fitger's profits were not generating a sufficient return on investment for the Fitger estate. In July 1951, the estate (known as the California Group) received an offer to purchase all of the company stock (including the minority interests, which were known as the Duluth Group) for $500,000. The prospective purchaser had no connection with Fitger's. When the Duluth Group, consisting of John Beerhalter, Walter Johnson, and Bert Jeronimus, learned of this, they felt that they should have been offered the first option to purchase the brewery. Eventually a deal was finalized in 1953 that transferred all stock from the California group to the Duluth Group.

The Duluth Group used most of the cash reserves of the corporation to purchase Fitger's. After the purchase there was not enough money left for improvements needed, so the group took out a large five-year loan. At this time, Beerhalter owned fifty-nine percent of the stock and the Johnson and Jeronimus interests owned forty-one percent.

Financial Pressures on Breweries

In the early 1950s, there were three breweries operating in Duluth and each one was experiencing a steady decline in sales. There was talk on the street that two of the brew-

eries should close and the remaining brewery should brew all three of the companies' beers in one plant. Mergers were becoming commonplace for breweries in the United

The boardroom in the early 1950s. John Beerhalter Sr. is seated at left; at right is Gus Buehring, a Fitger's salesman for over forty years. The pictures on either side of the painting above the fireplace are of August Fitger on the right and Percy Anneke on the left.

States. However, not one of the presidents was willing to give up his position.

Instead, the company presidents met to devise, for the first time, a combined marketing effort to increase sales in each of the breweries. The plan was an advertising program known as the "Three R's" representing the initials of the beers each sold: People's sold Regal, Duluth Brewing and Malting sold Royal 58, and Fitger's sold Rex Beer.

Fitger's continued to use "The Call of the North" advertising campaign in conjunction with the "Three R's." Its campaign featured outdoor recreation and nature. Many of the advertising products also featured a lighthouse with the phrase, "Brewed on the Shores of Lake Superior."

The joint marketing effort did not work and People's Brewery eventually closed in the mid-1950s. Fitger's continued its outdoor-themed advertising into the 1950s and 1960s, featuring wildlife and slogans such as "This is Fitgerland" and "Flavor of the Great North Shore."

A New Price Point Beer

Fitger's redoubled efforts to steer the brewery operation in the right direction. In the 1930s, it had introduced a price-point beer, Nordlager, which had been successful through the 1940s. In 1955, Fitger's decided to introduce another price point beer. Walter Johnson preferred the name Nordlager, which was already trademarked. However, it was

Fitger's continued to participate in Duluth parades as part of its advertising strategy.

finally decided to name the new price point beer "Twins Lager" to tie into the Twin Ports of Duluth and Superior and also the new baseball team, the Minnesota Twins. Twins Lager was very similar to the regular Fitger's beer, with the exception of being darker.

There were troubles other than declining sales. The declining profits negatively affected the employees' morale. Communication channels between some officers also began to break down. John Beerhalter Sr. passed away in 1955, and John Beerhalter Jr. became chairman as well as president of Fitger's. He and Walter Johnson had sat next to each other since Beerhalter Jr. had been named president in 1948. Communication between these two important officers eventually became non-existent, a sharp contrast to the earlier relationship between the senior Beerhalter and Johnson, who had worked very closely together for many years.

In the late 1950s, Fitger's had significant cash flow problems. To save money on labels, the brewery decided to get away from the names "Rex" and "Nordlager" and emphasize just the word "Fitger's." When Fitger's distributors requested some Rex or Nordlager, both of which had a loyal following in some areas, the brewery did not order any new large bottle labels for Rex or Nordlager, but just used small neck labels to identify them. As another cost-saving measure, Twins Lager was sold only in returnable pints at first. Eventually, it was sold in a throwaway bottle in an effort to compete with other non-returnable beers, but this cost the brewery more to purchase new bottles for each batch. Fitger's once again began selling Twins Lager in returnable bottles in an effort to save money.

In anticipation of introducing Twins Lager in cans, the brewery was able to purchase six-pack containers on credit, but they failed to find any company willing to extend credit for Twins Lager cans. The six-pack containers were stored upstairs in the bottle house for nearly fifteen years until the last president of Fitger's, John Ferris, purchased a semi load of Twin Lager cans and used some of them.

Financial Problems Get Worse

Fitger's tried to take advantage of a new shipping route created in 1960 with the opening of the St. Lawrence Seaway. Fitger's was able to convince the Dortmunder Brewery in Germany that shipping across the Atlantic and up the Seaway was cost effective and the purity of the beer would never be compromised because the ships had refrig-

A wildlife-themed calendar from 1967.

erated storage. Fitger's was the first brewery not on the East Coast to import Dortmunder Union Beer. Dortmunder was another quality product for Fitger's and did well, but was only a niche beer. Soon, the brewery had to call on distributors to pay in advance so beer orders could be brewed and bottled. In addition, the brewery no longer could offer credit to customers, further eroding sales. During the 1960s, Erwin Beerhalter, who now was vice-president, tried to arrange mergers with other breweries, especially in Canada, and Bert Jeronimus, the Treasurer, urged diversification into other products, but neither occurred.

Beer sales continued to decline, hampering Fitger's cash flow. At the same time the Minnesota Pollution Control Agency was ordering Fitger's to install approximately $100,000 worth of pollution control equipment and the Highway Department was considering using some or all of the brewery property for the extension of Interstate 35 in eastern Duluth. Duluth Brewing and Malting closed in 1966 when the State of Minnesota bought the brewing department portion of the property for interstate construction. The state paid $700,000 for the property through condemnation proceedings and construction began in August 1966 (some of the buildings were not demolished and are still standing today). There was a rumor at this time that the state would purchase

Fitger's Twins Lager Beer was eventually available in both cans and bottles.

Fitger's by eminent domain for Interstate 35 as well, which decreased sales at the brewery even more.

Fitger's was also losing market share to national breweries that engaged in extremely competitive price wars. Oftentimes, a brewery would canvas an area for two weeks, offering huge discounts to retailers in hopes that they would begin selling the brewery's beer and drop the competition's beer. Many of the accounts had a loyalty to Fitger's, but the price war was constant and Fitger's was unable to compete. Compared to Fitger's, the large companies had an unlimited supply of money, which they used to run the smaller breweries out of business. In addition, many of the people who had opened taverns after Prohibition and had a strong loyalty to Fitger's were retiring and selling to new owners who did not share the same loyalties.

The future of Fitger's was in severe jeopardy. At one point, Fitger's had to pay cash for a truckload of grain in

Fitger's Employees Still Had Fun

Beginning in the 1930s, Fitger's employee-organized Recreation Club sponsored sporting teams, planned holiday parties, and organized the company's annual picnics—and continued to do so into the mid-1960s. Author Coopen Johnson recalls:

"The picnics that I attended were at the Young Old-timers picnic grounds on the Cloquet River. Fitger's furnished all the pop and beer, and we had softball games between various departments. One thing I always remember about the picnics was the singing. John Hey, the former chemist at the brewery, would be one of the first to arrive at the picnic grounds. He would lead everyone in singing the 'Star Spangled Banner' at the flag-raising ceremony, but as soon as that was over, he'd jump in his car and go home."

The End of a Tap Room Tradition

The Tap Room had been available to rent for private parties for over twenty years for a mere $10 a night, including the bartender and an unlimited supply of beer.

In late 1960s, however, some enterprising students from UMD brought an end to that tradition. Students would rent the room under the guise of a club, pay the $10 fee, and then sell tickets to their friends for $1 per person. The sale of forty tickets would net them $30 in addition to having a beer party for free. Brewery officials learned of such violations, and thus ended the $10 Tap Room bargain.

The Tap Room was revived in the late 1980s as a bar and dance club with live music, but it is located in a different part of the complex (the original Tap Room was in the same space now occupied by the Snow Goose). It is once again popular among the college crowd.

Fitger's Tap Room in the 1960s.

order to make a batch of beer. Fitger's, following the lead of other breweries, decided to save money by using liquid hops rather than natural grain hops. Liquid hops, however, greatly reduced the shelf life of the beer, and if the beer became old, it tasted like vinegar. Some of the employees became very upset with this decision, because up to this time Fitger's had always used only the finest ingredients available. Some even refused to work in the bottle house.

The decision to use liquid hops was quickly reversed, but it had already tarnished Fitger's reputation and sales declined dramatically, forcing Fitger's to pull out of the Minneapolis market completely. Many loyal Fitger's customers became disgruntled and switched to other brands of beer.

Shake-up at Fitger's

In 1968, Richard Beerhalter's son Robert, a grandson of John Beerhalter Sr., was agent for his mother, who held the shares of her late husband. Robert joined with the minority shareholders to oust his uncles, John Jr. and Erwin, and take control of the Fitger Brewing Company. Robert

became president, but he also was a full-time dentist in Duluth and had no knowledge of the beer business. Because of his lack of experience, Fitger's decided to discontinue in-house distribution and subcontracted distribution to Coopen Johnson.

The summer of 1968 was cold and rainy, which was not conducive to the sale of beer, and 1969 sales were even worse, despite a long strike by the employees at all of the breweries in Milwaukee. Fitger's had hoped to capitalize on the strike by reducing wholesale prices to increase its market share, but this never occurred. Eventually there was no money to advertise, purchase supplies, or even pay employees. Robert Beerhalter needed money quickly and sold the land where the old ice house had stood to the Pickwick for some $30,000. (The land became a parking lot on the east side of the Pickwick.) The Pop Shop was closed without any attempt to sell the Squirt or Lovit franchises. Employee, distributor, and minority investor morale was low. Some distributors failed to pay their bills. The management started looking for a buyer for the brewery.

John Beerhalter Jr. (center) meets with a KDAL-TV representative in the Tap Room to introduce a new advertising plan.

Part V

Closings
and Openings

The Fitger's Complex as it stands today.

CHAPTER 18

The End of an Era

In July 1969, John Ferris became president of Fitger's. He and George G. Barnum entered into a complicated financial arrangement with the brewery that included having the Fitger's stockholders turn some of their stock over to a trust that was used as collateral for loans. The bank required reorganization to result in an even ten thousand shares of Fitger Brewing Company stock, so the corporation had a 33-to-1 split and bought back sixty-five shares from the seven Beerhalter shareholders at $20 per share for a total cash outlay of $1,300. Ferris also bought out the complete holdings of Cecile Beerhalter for about $40,000. Ferris and Barnum then loaned the corporation $120,000 for five years at ten percent interest, backed by a second mortgage on Fitger's property. First Bank of Duluth held another mortgage from a 1963 loan that had already been extended.

After all this reorganization, the company that had been purchased for $500,000 in 1951, and then immediately mortgaged for a substantial amount of that, now had ten thousand shares valued at $200,000, a new $120,000 loan from Ferris and Barnum, and the old mortgage as well. Cash flow continued to be a very precarious situation.

Ferris was a very astute businessperson and had a firm handle on all the costs and expenses involved at Fitger's, but he had no experience in many of the areas required to successfully compete in the beer market. By the end of 1969, the balance sheet had dropped from $250,000 to approximately $5,000. By the spring of 1970, more money was needed. Although the officers had estimated that the Fitger's shares would be valued between $12 and $15 a share just six months earlier, an audit of the books put the value at forty-nine cents per share. A minority shareholder report on February 3, 1970, accused the officers of raiding corporate assets by selling the land and building to the Pickwick, closing the Pop Shop without selling the Squirt and Lovit franchises, and failing to hire the appropriate management and staff to revitalize the brewery operations and sales.

Shortly afterward, Ferris purchased additional shares from the Beerhalter heirs at ninety-nine cents per share. In the case of Erwin Beerhalter, Ferris paid $996 for 1,006 shares, which, added to the $40 for two shares six months earlier, was the only payment received for nearly fifteen percent of Fitger's stock. While the Beerhalters still retained small holdings, they would never receive any further compensation for their shares. Ferris also promised to extend personal funds to the brewery in exchange for the brewery-owned distributorship buildings in Virginia and Bemidji and, if necessary, mortgages against other real and personal property of Fitger's. One by one, the employees began to leave Fitger's and seek other employment. Many of the bottle house employees found jobs at the University of Minnesota Duluth, which was adding to its existing campus at the time. Otto Becker, the brewmaster, went to work for Anheuser-Busch.

There were rumors among the employees that the only reason Ferris bought the brewery was to benefit financially when the Minnesota Highway Department bought the brewery for Interstate 35. But Ferris's father, a Boston banker, had taken Pilgrim Laundries (a company on the verge of bankruptcy) picked it up, put some money into it, and sold it for a good profit. Ferris felt he could do the same with Fitger's. After only a short period of time, he realized the buildings were outmoded, and the brewing business was altogether different than the laundry business. Despite this, Ferris managed to eventually pay off all of the debt that Fitger's had incurred.

Fitger's Closes After Ninety-One Years

Ferris continued to deal with the State of Minnesota regarding the two significant situations that arose before his involvement in Fitger's. The deadline for compliance with the Minnesota Pollution Control Agency's order for the installation of pollution abatement equipment had been extended several times due to the uncertainty of the State Highway Department plans for routing the extension of Interstate 35 through the brewery. Ferris also kept receiving letters from the Highway Department stating that it was interested in at least some of the brewery's property, but that a final decision would not be made until an uncertain date in the future.

Finally, the Minnesota Pollution Control Agency sent a letter to Ferris in mid-September 1972, citing a stipula-

Sign-in sheet for the bottle house workers (left) and brew house canning workers (right) on the final day of canning.

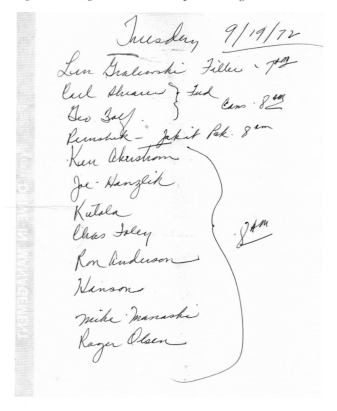

tion agreement "either to complete an expensive pollution abatement project or close down...not later than September 30, 1972." In the same week, Fitger's received a letter from State Highway Commissioner Ray Lappagard that said although final alignment of the freeway had not been determined, "It appears that it would be impractical for you to install pollution abatement facilities in view of the planning currently in process regarding the possible extension of I-35 within the city of Duluth."

Ferris issued a news release stating he had made the decision not to comply with the MPCA stipulation because "brewery property is included in present plans for extension of Interstate 35 and it is not practical to make a substantial investment in pollution abatement if the buildings are to be acquired by the State Highway Department for right-of-way. Such an investment, if made, would only increase state and federal costs for acquiring Fitger property and would temporarily limit our ability to invest in other job-producing enterprises." Ferris concluded, "It is with deep regret that we are forced to suspend operations and lay off many loyal employees." Only five employees would remain, including Ferris and his wife, to close down the brewery and then maintain the plant at minimal levels. Fifteen employees, eight of whom had twenty or more years of service with Fitger's, were let go. The last beer was brewed August 14, 1972, the last bottling was done on September 14, and the last canning followed on September 19. Ferris and his six-person staff dismantled everything of value from the brewery, including beautiful redwood aging tanks, oak-fermenting tanks, and oak settling and finishing tanks. All of these items eventually were sold to other breweries, companies, and individuals. It was very disheartening for many of the people who had been involved with Fitger's in one way or another to see these items leave the brewery forever.

Ferris contracted with Schell's Brewery in New Ulm, Minnesota, to produce and distribute Fitger's Beer, which it

The Fitger's Brewery, locked and gated after operations closed.

did until 1984. Ferris had announced plans to build a new warehouse on a two-acre site in the new Duluth Airport Industrial Park for distributing both Fitger's and Schell's products. The warehouse was never built. Later in 1972, Ferris purchased sixty percent of Fitger's stock from Northwestern National Bank of Minneapolis. It is not known what Ferris paid to purchase the stock.

Fitger's Escapes the Wrecking Ball

The extension of I-35 from Mesaba Avenue to Twenty-sixth Avenue East and London Road was a federal highway project with the objective of extending the freeway at the least possible cost. The original plans of the project nearly eliminated all access to the shore of Lake Superior and several historic buildings would have been razed. This

and other issues concerned many Duluthians, and a Duluth citizen's committee was formed to address them.

There was a growing call to preserve Fitger's. The *Duluth News-Tribune* noted on February 22, 1976, "The Fitger Brewing Company buildings on Superior Street seem destined for destruction under a plan to extend Interstate 35 to its vicinity." The paper went on to quote Minnesota State Preservation Officer Russell Fridley:

"The structure should be saved. It is eligible for inclusion in the National Register of Historic Places. It is one of the last examples of an early American brewery left in the state. It has a very unique architecture and the materials that went into its construction make the structure an extremely distinctive building. If we do not have the persuasive power to preserve the building, I hope the citizens

Brewing equipment and a wooden beer case left abandoned in the brewery after it closed.

of Duluth would become concerned over losing what they have—a city with several buildings and homes of historical and architectural significance along a proposed I-35 corridor between Mesaba Avenue and 26th Avenue East."

Fridley was quoted as saying that if the Fitger buildings faced demolition, the Department of Interior's National Advisory Council on Historic Preservation had the power to prevent the demise and force highway construction to another corridor. Three buildings in addition to the Fitger's complex were of particular concern to the citizens' committee.

District Highway Engineer John Pawlack said three of the buildings of concern to the committee—October House No. 1, the Hartley Building, and the Endion Railway Depot—could be moved, if necessary, but

Fitger's could not because of the number and size of the buildings. A month later, the Citizens committee recommended an alternate route north of Fitger's. Two years later, that plan was approved and acquisition of the required land began. The freeway swung north to preserve Fitger's Brewery, the Pickwick, October House No. 1, and the Hartley Building. Endion Station was moved.

Fitger's Sues the State

In 1978, the Fitger Brewing Company sued the State of Minnesota for damages relating to the forced closing of the brewery and also for the loss of rail access and the restriction of truck access to the plant. The new route would dismantle the railroad spur leading to Fitger's and would eliminate Fifth Avenue East and Michigan Street access to the

Wooden kegs, not used for decades before the brewery closed, remained behind after closing.

yard behind the Superior Street buildings. The suit called for $2.5 million in actual damages and also argued that state actions had diminished the value of the property; Fitger's used the theory of "inverse condemnation," which sought damages the same as if formal condemnation procedures had been followed. It was the first time inverse condemnation had been part of a lawsuit in Minnesota.

No progress had been made in negotiations with the state since the closing of the brewery, and now the state proposed compensation only for the loss of the railroad spur and the Fifth Avenue East and Michigan Street corner of the Fitger property. John Ferris and the Fitger's Board of Directors were responsible for maintaining a huge, mostly

unused complex of buildings that was rapidly deteriorating—it would not be taken by the state, and there was a citizens' proposal for preservation of the buildings. Eventually, historic designation seemed likely for Fitger's.

Fitger's board of directors was first advised that any sale of the property could interfere with the lawsuit against the state. But in 1979 attorneys told the directors that they could seek other uses for the property without jeopardizing the suit. Ferris was authorized to act for the board. That same year, Minneapolis developer Ron Jacob, who was also developing a former mattress factory into the Nicollet Island Inn in Minneapolis, first toured the Fitger's property.

The tunnel leading to what is now the Tap Room, neglected and damp while the complex sat vacant.

CHAPTER 19

New Life for an Old Brewery

Ron Jacob was fascinated with the potential for Fitger's Brewery renovation. When the Fitger's Board of Directors finally received new legal advice that a sale of the property would not jeopardize the suit against the State of Minnesota, negotiations began. Jacob's first partnership attempt to buy the brewery was headed by Minneapolis developer Alan Fischlowitz and included Minneapolis businesswoman Beth Ferrell. In May 1981 the group announced that it expected to reach an agreement to purchase the property by October 1, 1981. They envisioned a forty-room hotel with restaurant, meeting, and banquet facilities in the former bottle house; a restaurant and specialty retail complex of about 60,000 square feet in the former stock houses, engine and boiler houses, wash house, and racking room; and 6,300 square feet of commercial space in the former Pop Shop, for a total cost of $12 million to $15 million. On September 25, 1981, the *Duluth Herald* quoted Fischlowitz as saying they would seek designation on the National Register of Historic Places for Fitger's, which would qualify the project for grants and tax incentives, and they would also apply for other financing from public and private sources. The deal never materialized.

Jacob Tries Again

Financing for the massive project was troublesome, but Jacob did not give up. Next, he enlisted the help of Minneapolis lawyer Jack Helms, who was a specialist in real estate development.

Planning had long been underway even before the actual purchase, and a gala presentation was held February 18, 1983, to announce the redevelopment plan to the public. Lieutenant Governor Marlene Johnson represented the State of Minnesota at the ribbon cutting ceremonies. Duluth Mayor John Fedo applauded the "new partnership between the developers and the city on a project that should add to the revitalization of downtown Duluth," according to the *Duluth News-Tribune & Herald* (the two papers had merged in 1982). The newspaper estimated that more than 250 people attended the ceremonies and slide presentation in the former Silver Spray Gym, which is the main entrance to the Fitger's Complex today.

This was the first major attempt at historical redevelopment for the City of Duluth. Prior to the Fitger's project, Duluth had focused its economic development on new construction, such as the Radisson and Holiday Inn hotels. Later, the city would be involved with both historic and new development in the Canal Park area and downtown Duluth.

The Brewery Limited Partnership announced plans for a $9.5 million project including forty to forty-seven hotel rooms, 20,000 to 30,000 square feet of retail space for small specialty shops, and several restaurants. Key attractions would include a minibrewery, a museum, and a multi-media theater, which could also be used for conferences and seminars, an unusual combination for historic redevelopments at that time. The Duluth newspaper quoted Helms on the short-term and long-term economic benefits of the Fitger's project as including up to 130 full-time construction jobs for Duluth labor and a payroll of more than $2 million a year for about 250 permanent jobs. The developers hoped to start remodeling in the fall and open by June 1984 for the full summer tourist season. Financing, however, would delay the timetable again.

To secure sufficient investor equity to convince Minneapolis banks to guarantee government bond issues, Helms found a new partner to buy out his and Jacob's first six limited partners—some of whom retained an ownership in the separate Fitger's Inn partnership, which was created to manage and operate the Fitger Inn and its restaurant. The new partner was Pemble & Associates, comprised of Clyde Pemble, Craig Chittum, and William Harrison. Helms told the *News-Tribune & Herald,* "They brought us respect." The Pemble group also brought professional construction-project management to the partnership.

After several months of extensive planning and negotiation, Brewery Limited Partnership put together a complex financial package. The partnership contributed about $2 million in equity. First National Bank of Minneapolis agreed to back $4.85 million in U.S. Industrial Development Revenue Bonds and another one million in tax increment financing bonds. The City

of Duluth was also seeking a federal Housing and Urban Development (HUD) Action Grant of more than $3 million to build a parking ramp to serve the retail complex. Negotiations on the federal portions went beyond the original July 1, 1983, goal for start of construction.

A Bump in the Road

On September 19, 1983, HUD indicated it would not approve the parking ramp grant because it did not directly provide permanent jobs. Without adequate parking, the restaurant and retail complex could not be expected to prosper; the entire Fitger's project was in jeopardy. Eventually the city loaned the partnership the money needed to build the parking ramp.

Construction was delayed several months but finally started late 1983. It was a daunting task. Cleanup of the vandalized and bird-infested structure was the first item on the agenda. Then came remodeling. New tiled walkways curved through the inside of the building to carry shoppers through the two-level shopping arcade. Many fixtures were left exposed to accentuate the original industrial nature of the complex. Fitger's memorabilia and pictures were displayed on the old brick and stone walls. The copper kettle became the focal point of the new museum. The lobby at Fitger's Inn featured some of the original grillwork as well as the beautiful bank vault door, the original ornate skylight and grand two-story columns, and the original entryway and window openings. Fitger's was ready to reopen in December 1984—six months behind schedule.

Fitger's on the Lake

Fitger's on the Lake had missed the summer tourist season, but opened just in time for the end of the holiday shopping season. The new Fitger's was greeted with fanfare and great interest among Duluthians who had been hearing about the project for several years.

The initial enthusiasm was blunted, however, by highway construction just two years later in 1986. Interstate 35 construction was finally underway and the tunneling project in front of Fitger's left a massive trench next to the new retail complex and hotel, leaving no vehicle access along Superior Street. In addition, the constant dirt and noise negatively affected Fitger's Inn, the hotel restaurant, and the retail stores. Brewery Limited Partnership filed for Chapter 11 bankruptcy protection in December 1987 after the major creditor, First Bank of Minneapolis, asked the court to appoint a receiver because of missed payments. The Partnership also owed the City of Duluth for the parking ramp loan and unpaid property taxes. Brewery Limited Partnership sued the State of Minnesota to recover damages for loss of cus-

tomers, but the suit failed. Fitger's on the Lake continued to struggle for nearly two more years before a former Duluthian stepped in to help.

Papaik takes over Fitger's on the Lake

In late September 1989, William Papaik—a graduate of Duluth's Morgan Park High School—and two other partners contracted to purchase Fitger's on the Lake for $5.5 million from First National Bank of Minneapolis. They would never actually own the complex.

Papaik owned various hotel properties, including the Chequamegon Hotel in Ashland, Wisconsin, and Telemark Lodge in Cable, Wisconsin. He was also a partner in over sixty strip malls and also nearly forty Children's Palace toy stores. Papaik had the experience required to manage Fitger's.

A portion of the fortress-like Fitger's Complex, the mill house (built in 1900) as it looks today.

With the responsibility of all his holdings, Papaik was stretched thin. Bob Greenly, vice president of Telemark Development, was given the duty of developing a management team for Fitger's. He selected George Hovland III as the property's general manager. Hovland worked for Papaik as manager of the Telemark Lodge and Papaik felt he was the perfect candidate to manage Fitger's.

In 1989 Superior Street was still not completed, continuing to adversely affect the complex's hotel and retail shops. Hovland was responsible for the retail tenants, the Tap Room, the hotel, and Augustino's restaurant. At first the restaurant did extremely well. Chef Glenn D'amour was renowned in the region and had developed a strong local following.

The success of the hotel—which had been profitable before Papaik arrived—was undermined by increased competition from the new hotels sprouting up in Duluth's Canal Park, an area undergoing its own renovation. Fitger's dropped rates to $50 a night and included a free continental breakfast, hoping to lure guests from the new hotels and downtown's Radisson and Holiday Inn.

Papaik promised many changes to assist the retail tenants. Business was slow throughout the area and traffic counts in Fitger's were much lower due to Superior Street being closed for highway expansion. The changes never occurred and tenants eventually became disenchanted. Many did not renew their leases when they expired. This left many spaces vacant and reduced traffic within the mall even more.

The winter of 1991–1992 proved to be the final nail in the coffin for Papaik. Fitger's as an individual entity may have survived these difficult times. But the deal Papaik negotiated with his bank was highly leveraged and did not allow cash flow to be reinvested in the property. In addition, nearly all of the profit Fitger's did generate was directed towards some of Papaik's other holdings, which were having financial difficulties of their own.

Even though the large complex had been completely remodeled, it still needed constant maintenance and repair. Papaik simply did not have the funds and Fitger's entered into receivership for the second time. Fitger's had a commanding presence overlooking Lake Superior and both the Duluth and Superior entries. It was also situated adjacent to the new Lakewalk, a favorite destination for both tourists and local residents. Eventually new investors would be found who believed that Fitger's was the jewel of Duluth and could be a very successful operation.

Fitger's Inn and Brewery Complex

On June 12, 1991, Scott Vesterstein, the owner of the Benetton clothing store in Fitger's, contacted Towle Realty in Minneapolis to discuss buying the Fitger's complex from First Bank, the mortgage holder of the property. Fitger's was being managed by Andy Andrews of Regency Inns, which also had an interest in purchasing the property.

Fitger's had seen a continual decline in occupied retail space that was adversely affecting the remaining tenants in the mall. Much of the vacant space was being used for storage, creating unsightly black spaces within the corridors. Augustino's restaurant was also having financial problems. During these difficult times the hotel continued to be profitable, although many necessary improvements had been put on hold until a buyer could be found.

Vesterstein had seen some of Fitger's darkest days but also saw great potential. He put together a revitalization plan including five goals:

1. Increase the number of hotel rooms from forty-eight to sixty to decrease per-room costs.
2. Find a quality food and beverage operator for the space vacated by Rocky Rococco.

Opposite: Fitger's smokestack and water tower remain as landmarks to this day, standing in the lakefront courtyard area of Fitger's Complex. When the partners of Fitger's-on-the-Lake LLC took over the property, they recognized that developing interest in the complex's history was the key to its future success. Among the changes they made was to have a version of the Fitger's logo painted on the water tower.

3. Design a more inviting entrance from the parking ramp into the mall.

4. Provide Lakewalk access to the mall courtyard.

5. Feature the history of Fitger's.

During the receivership, the historical theme of the mall had been replaced with a Lake Superior theme. Giant sepia prints of former Fitger's employees, which had been mounted on the mall walls, were taken down and replaced with paint. Vesterstein believed the history of Fitger's was the main attraction of the complex and would change the theme back and build a museum filled with Fitger's memorabilia.

On January 14, 1994, Fitger's-on-the-Lake LLC became the new owner of the complex. The partnership consisted of Scott Vesterstein, Paul Vesterstein, Carolyn Vesterstein, Ron Johnson, Vlasie Solon, Jack Thomas, John Ethen, and Ron and Mary Ann Weber. John Ethen, who relocated to Montana, was bought out by the partnership in 1995. Plans began immediately to add twelve more hotel suites, build the Fitger's Station to provide access to the lakewalk, and construct a new west entrance. New tenants were recruited to the complex to lease the vacant space. Shear Katz Salon and Day Spa, Fitger's Brewhouse, and many other retail stores, restaurants, and offices opened in Fitger's.

In 1997 Bennett's restaurant, located at 319 West Superior Street, formerly the Black Steer building, moved to Fitger's, replacing Augustino's restaurant. The partnership felt it was best to get someone such as Bob Bennett to operate and own the hotel restaurant. Bob was renowned as a first-class chef and, along with his wife, Kathy, added the fine-dining element Fitger's needed for hotel guests and other customers.

As of summer 2004, The Snow Goose, owned by Kris Kauzlaric, is the only original businesses remaining since Fitger's 1984 reopening. Benetton has been open since 1985.

Today Fitger's is a thriving renovated 1881 brewery featuring four restaurants, a variety of wonderful specialty stores, two nightclubs, and various banquet facilities. Fitger's Inn, Duluth's only four-diamond hotel, now has sixty-two rooms and suites. Fitger's is one of Duluth's most precious landmarks and continues to be a favorite destination for tourists and Duluthians alike.

Original Lawsuit Finally Settled

The State of Minnesota had fought the right of Fitger's to sue in 1980, but the Minnesota Supreme Court ordered the district court to hear Fitger's 1978 suit on its merits. The case did not go to the jury until November 1986.

Fitger's attorney William O'Brien argued that the state had effectively taken the property. The jury agreed and awarded more than $2 million, before subtracting $700,000 for the 1983 sale of the property and another several hundred thousand for rent received between 1972 and 1983. O'Brien then sued for interest, and the district court increased the total award to $5.6 million by using average bond rates during that period of high rates to calculate the interest. The state had indicated it supported an award for about half as much interest, opening the door to possible negotiation in lieu of the state filing an appeal. But O'Brien said Ferris was adamant.

The state appealed and received a complete reversal from the Minnesota Supreme Court in 1987. The proceeds from the 1983 sale went to paying back salaries for Ferris and his wife, Claire; for overdue property taxes; and for other business expenses. No shareholders received any compensation from the sale.

CHAPTER 20

Brewing Returns to Fitger's

In the winter of 1994, the Lake Superior Brewing Company had begun brewing small batches of beer in the Fitger's Complex, becoming Duluth's first commercial brewery since Fitger's Brewing Company closed in 1972. It was an inauspicious beginning for the small brewery and home-brew supply shop; the company only brewed on Sundays, producing six-barrel batches using dairy equipment. The beer was only available on draught in Duluth and Superior. Within six months, however, the company had moved to a larger space in Fitger's, quadrupling in square footage. It began brewing eight-barrel batches and selling beer in small two-and-a-quarter-gallon kegs called "Party Pigs."

Fitger's Brewhouse

In September 1995, the Fitger's Brewhouse opened its doors in the former Rocky Rococco restaurant space, fulfilling a goal Scott Vesterstein had pursued for over three years. The Brewhouse was not a microbrewery, but a restaurant offering pub fare and many vegetarian options. The Brewhouse would be the first restaurant in town to offer Lake Superior Brewing Company beers to its customers.

Brewhouse bartender Mike Hoops, an avid home brewer, also volunteered as an apprentice at Lake Superior Brewing. After a year or two steeped in hands-on education, Hoops convinced Brewhouse owners Tim Nelson and Rod Raymond he was ready to operate his own brewery. The Brewhouse began its first expansion.

Hoops found used equipment for the Brewhouse's original English-style brewery in Colorado and drove it back to Duluth in a rented truck. The Brewhouse served its own beer, a strong dark brew called "Petroglyph Porter," for the first time in April 1997. Lake Superior Brewing Company also had plans for expansion, and moved to a larger site in July 1998, where it still brews today. This vacated space allowed the Brewhouse to expand further. In the late 1990s, the Brewhouse was making 300 barrels of six or seven varieties of beer per year—and winning awards for it. At the annual Taste of the Midwest brew pub festival in Madison, Wisconsin, Hoops' recipes for Witch Tree ESB, Big Boat Oatmeal Stout, and some of his lambic beers began taking home gold and silver medals and did so for several years to come.

The Brewhouse continued to grow. Soon its taps poured seven in-house varieties of beer at a time, and the

Fitger's Brewhouse: An Award-Winning Tradition

The Brewhouse has won many awards for its beers, including:

1998 Taste of the Midwest
Gold—Witch Tree ESB

Gold—Big Boat Oatmeal Stout

1999 Taste of the Midwest
Gold—Witch Tree ESB

Silver—Apricot Wheat

Silver—Jessie the Barleywine

2000 Taste of the Midwest
Gold—El Nino IPA

Silver—Hair O' the Monk

Silver—Witch Tree ESB

Bronze—Starfire Pale Ale

2001 Taste Of the Midwest
Gold—Starfire Pale Ale

Gold—Watermelon Wheat

Silver—Breakwater White

2002 Taste of the Midwest (Final Year)
Gold—Witch Tree ESB

Silver—Big Boat Oatmeal Stout

Silver—El Nino IPA

Silver—Edmund Imperial Stout

Bronze—Farmhouse Ale

2003 Winterfest Strong Beer Festival, St. Paul, Minnesota
Best Beer—Hair O' the Monk

2004 Great American Beer Festival (Denver)
Bronze—Farmhouse Reserve Saison

brewery was producing more than thirty different beers. After several years, Mike Hoops left the Brewhouse to eventually become the head brewer at the Town Hall brew pub in Minneapolis. Luckily for Nelson and Raymond, Mike had an older brother, Dave.

Dave Hoops had been working as the lead brewer at the Pyramid Brewery in Berkeley, California. Dave's background was similar to Mike's: a home brewer who traded time at local breweries in exchange for an education. But Dave took it a step further and attended Chicago's Seibel Institute of Technology for a six-month brewing program that included an apprenticeship at, in Dave's case, Goose Island Brewery. Dave started making beer for the Brewhouse late in 1999.

Soon after Dave Hoops' arrival, the Brewhouse was producing over 700 barrels a year and continued to expand its brewing capacity. But in 2001, fire struck the brewery. The fail-safe on the Brewhouse's electric kettle failed, and the kettle caught fire. The fire became the impetus for more growth. A bar was removed from one of the Brewhouse's dining rooms and the space was used to build a larger, two-level brewery that included walk-in refrigeration for the finished beers and six conditioning tanks that allow the beer to age properly. That expansion also increased production to over 1,000 barrels a year. By 2003 production had reached the new system's capacity, so in 2004 the Brewhouse added four more tanks—two new fermenters to brew more beer on a weekly basis and two new tanks for conditioning—raising the capacity to 1,400 barrels a year. The Brewhouse became the number-two producer of brew pub beer by volume in Minnesota, second only to the franchised Rock Bottom Brewery in downtown Minneapolis.

On any given day, the Brewhouse offers twelve different beers on tap, two on nitrogen, one on the English hand-pump, and special beers made in small batches and wood casked (bourbon aged). In 2003, the Brewhouse produced fifty-eight distinct beers. Hoops credits the people of Duluth with the Brewhouse's variety, because local folks seem more than willing to try everything the Brewhouse makes, from traditional pale ales to fruit-based lambics to challenging Scotch ales.

The Brewhouse was also instrumental in changing Minnesota legislation. Before 2003, Minnesota brew pubs could not sell beer in containers to be consumed outside of the restaurant. Dave Hoops and other Minnesota brewers set up the nonprofit Minnesota Craft Brewer's Guild and raised money to lobby the Senate in St. Paul to change the law. After four years of hard work, including testimony from Tim Nelson, a bill was passed in August 2003 allowing Minnesota brew pubs to sell growlers—jugs that hold four pints of beer—to go. Within a few months of the Brewhouse selling growlers, its beer sales increased twenty-five percent. The next step, says Hoops, is selling kegs.

The Brewhouse brewing crew's award-winning efforts continued into Fall 2004, at the time of this book's completion. Fitger's Brewhouse was awarded a bronze medal in Denver, Colorado, at the Great American Brew Festival, the world's largest brewery competition which recognizes what is considered the pinna-

The A. Fitger and Company Lake Superior Brewery doorway lintel of the 1886 stock house can be seen today outside Fitger's Brewhouse although the doorway itself has been filled in with bricks.

cle of brewery excellence. In the 2004 competition, 2,016 beers were judged and 201 medals handed out. Association of Brewers President Charlie Papazian awarded Dave Hoops and his assistants Frank Kaszuba and Andy Scheidel a bronze medal in the Belgian Beer category for their work making Farmhouse Special Reserve Saison. Brewed with coriander, ginger, grains of paradise, and orange peel, the beer is just one of Hoop's many creations.

The Hoops brothers also made Brew Festival history at the 2004 event as the first pair of brothers ever to win awards in the same year. Mike took home three silver medals for Town Hall—one for Scotch ale, one for strong Belgian, and one for honey ale. No other brewer won more.

As Fitger's Brewhouse beers continue to win awards, the Fitger's tradition of brewing on the shores of Lake Superior appears destined to continue for years to come.

The Fitger's Brewhouse crew: (from left) Assistants Andy Scheidel and Frank Kaszuba with Master Brewer Dave Hoops.

CHAPTER 21

Grain to Glass: Fitger's Brewing Process

The first steps in the Fitger's Brewery beer-making process started in the brew house and mill house, commonly called just the brew house. The grains were stored in bulk form in huge tanks. To begin the brewing process, the grains were weighed and placed in a large pressure cooker. These grains were transferred to the lauter tub (via gravity) where they formed a "floor" in the tub. The agitator, with the aid of much water, created a liquid known as "wort." The mash, now called "spent grains," went into a dryer and was then placed in 100-pound sacks to be sold to farmers for animal feed. The grant, which directed the wort from the lauter tub to the kettle, had fif-

---

From Mash to Wort

"To serve you a sparkling, clean, palatable, zestful glass of beer, calls for great skill, complete control, chemically and biologically, and a never-ending process of cleaning, disinfecting as well as sterilizing.

"The essential materials used in beer are Malt, Malt adjuncts, Hops, Yeast and biologically clean water. Eight definite steps are the fundamentals of the art of brewing.

"First, cooking the mash, which is a malt barley product, and the malt adjunct, which may be rice or corn. The malt supplies peptase and diastase, two substances which change the nature of certain other constituents during mashing. The adjuncts contain very little protein and are used mainly to produce a paler, lighter 'bodied' beer. Cooking loosens and softens the hard, flinty condition of the starch.

"Next, mashing the grain—to allow the starch to be converted into Maltose. The clear liquid, called wort, is taken off the grain—sent to the kettle and boiled. (The spent grain is used for cattle feed.) Boiling the 'wort' precipitates the undesirable proteins—thus making the wort clear and transparent. Domestic and imported hops are added to the kettle. Hops impart the fine aroma found in beer, due to the delicate esters and oils."

— John Beerhalter, Sr. "How Fitger's Fine Beer is Brewed"

teen openings with attached hoses that went to different sections and depths of the kettle. This was a quality-assurance process so that when the hops were added to the kettle they would mix evenly with the wort.

The grant was tapped three times and the hops were added every fifteen minutes. The whole brewing process took nine-and-a-half hours. Kenny Akerstrom thoroughly cleaned the dozen pie-shaped plates in the lauter tub after every brew. In addition to bi-weekly polishing of the outside of the copper kettle, the inside of the kettle had to be recoated once a year. The kettle man for decades was John Gressman, who died tragically in an accident at the brewery. Gressman was coating the inside of the aging tank, which required wearing a mask for protection from the sealant fumes. When someone accidentally fired-up the

The grant directing wort into the boiling kettle.

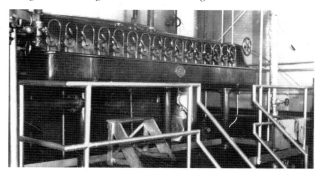

kettle before Gressman was finished with the coating, the fumes ignited and fatally injured him. After Gressman's death, Warren Young took over his position. Young would get to the brewery in the wee hours of the morning to start the kettle. When the hops were added, the mixture was heated for hours. When it was finished, the wort would go through a hops strainer. The hops strainer would catch the spent hop leaf, and the wort was then pumped to the top level of the stock house.

The Stock Houses

The wort first went to the cooling tanks above the Yeast Room, where it remained to cool down for approximately twenty-four hours. The wort was then drained over cooling plates, providing additional cooling before the yeast was added. Once the yeast was added, the liquid became beer.

The new beer was pumped into the fermenting cellars to ferment for ten days to two weeks. Although called "cellars," the fermenting tanks were actually several stories above the basement. During the fermenting process, naturally occurring carbon dioxide was allowed to escape for safety reasons. Some of the carbon dioxide was recaptured in tanks and was later put back into the beer in the finishing cellar to provide natural carbonation. Today, many brewers use nitrogen instead of natural carbonation to create the foam in beer.

From Aeration to Carbonation

"Aeration and cooling must follow quickly; 6,500 gallons are cooled through modern methods of refrigeration within 90 minutes. A pure cultured yeast, absolutely clean biologically, is added and the wort is sent to the Fermenting Cellars. Constant care of temperatures is essential to obtain uniformity. Germ-killing rays maintain pure air in these cellars at the Fitger Brewing Company.

"After fermenting, the beer is stored in huge vats to allow it to dry properly and age. When the beer has reached the proper age and has been subjected to periodic biological examinations it is then filtered several times and carbonated. At Fitger's the CO_2 gas given off by the fermenting process is compressed and used—thus no foreign taste is imparted; it leaves the finished product as natural as possible."

— John Beerhalter, Sr. "How Fitger's Fine Beer is Brewed"

Ready for Keg or Bottle

"Now the beer is ready to be sent to the Keg Room or to be bottled in the Bottling Department with modern up-to-date machinery. Bottle beer is pasteurized—thus insuring quality above all else."

— John Beerhalter, Sr.
"How Fitger's Fine Beer is Brewed"

After fermenting, the beer would go through hoses down to the second floor of the building into storage tanks to be aged for three or four weeks.

The yeast that had settled in the fermenting tanks would have grown two to three times in volume compared to the original amount of yeast. Yeast settling to the bottom is lager; yeast settling to the top is ale. The yeast remains were taken out, and the good yeast was used for the next batch of beer, while the excess yeast was used to polish the kettle. Many brew house workers would take a teaspoon or two per day of liquid yeast. They felt it was a good blood builder.

The beer went through the Kieselguhr filter after the aging process and from there the beer went into finishing tanks. Finally, the beer went through a polishing filter, making sure the beer was crystal clear. brew house employees checked the batches for quality before the beer was pumped to the government meter for measurement. From the government cellar, the beer was piped to the racking room to be put into kegs or to the bottle house to be put into cans or bottles.

The Racking Room

In the racking room, one man would fill the kegs and one man would pile the kegs. The job of piling was relatively simple but the job of filling was a little more complicat-

Fitger's redwood aging tanks.

A Flow Chart for the Brewing Process at Fitger's Brewery

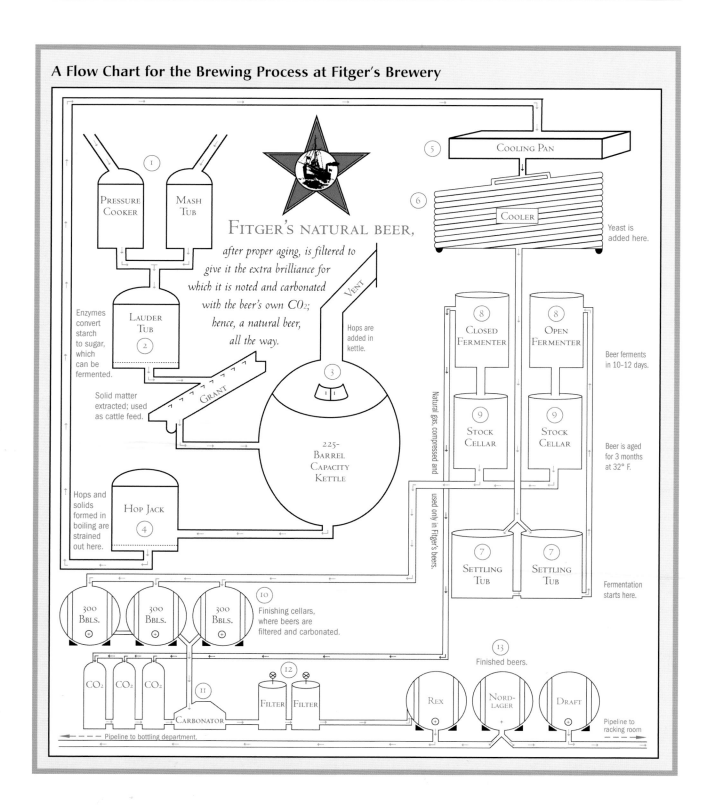

FITGER'S NATURAL BEER, *after proper aging, is filtered to give it the extra brilliance for which it is noted and carbonated with the beer's own CO2; hence, a natural beer, all the way.*

PRESSURE COOKER

MASH TUB

1

LAUDER TUB
2

Enzymes convert starch to sugar, which can be fermented.

Solid matter extracted; used as cattle feed.

GRANT

VENT

Hops are added in kettle.

3

225- BARREL CAPACITY KETTLE

HOP JACK
4

Hops and solids formed in boiling are strained out here.

COOLING PAN
5

COOLER
6

Yeast is added here.

CLOSED FERMENTER
8

OPEN FERMENTER
8

Beer ferments in 10-12 days.

STOCK CELLAR
9

STOCK CELLAR
9

Beer is aged for 3 months at 32° F.

Natural gas, compressed and used only in Fitger's beers.

SETTLING TUB
7

SETTLING TUB
7

Fermentation starts here.

300 BBLS.

300 BBLS.

300 BBLS.

Finishing cellars, where beers are filtered and carbonated.
10

13

Finished beers.

CO2

CO2

CO2

CARBONATOR
11

FILTER FILTER
12

REX

NORD-LAGER

DRAFT

Pipeline to racking room

Pipeline to bottling department.

ed. A cylindrical glass on the filler would get foamy as the keg was filled and became a pure amber color when it was full. After the keg was full, a five-pound mallet was used to knock in the plug, known as a "bung." Every keg of beer that left the racking room had to be stamped. This was one of the duties of the yardmen. Usually the kegs went out in lots of fifty at a time, so a five-step process had to be repeated fifty times. First, the men brushed an adhesive around the area where the keg was to be tapped; second, they placed the state stamp over the adhesive; third, the process was repeated for the federal stamp; fourth, a huge tack-like device was used to perforate the date into the stamps and then cancel them out; and, finally, all this was embedded into the cork. State and federal stamps had the dates perforated in the brewery office. By the mid-1960s the stamps were no longer used.

The Bottle House Step-by-Step

Step One: Three workers fed the soaker by removing empties from cases and putting each bottle into a compartment that slowly elevated to the main level of the bottle house. Emptied cases were sent via conveyor belt to the top floor of the bottle house to be cleaned. Step Two: After the labels were soaked off, the bottles were transferred via conveyor to the bottle washer for cleaning. Step Three: The bottles were inspected then filled and crowned. Step Four: The bottled beer was pasteurized, then run through the labeling machine. Step Five: A packer put the bottled beer back into cases. Cases arrived via chute from the top floor, where they had been cleaned. The filled cases were stored on the main floor until sold.

It took approximately one hour and fifteen minutes from the initial task to the final packing.

The racking room. The copper cylinder hanging from the ceiling held the beer waiting to be kegged.

Delivering the Beer, and Everything Else: The Yardmen

Most of the workers at the brewery spent their entire careers at Fitger's. Many even stayed in the same department. Each worker's schedule varied depending on the brewing and bottling cycle, because not every task was performed every day. Some activities varied by the season. Probably the widest variety of work came to the yardmen, who worked both outdoors and indoors at the brewery.

Fitger's hired additional help during the busy summer season, when beer sales would reach their peak. The extra help worked with the yardmen. Depending on the day, during the summer a yardman could find himself helping out on a truck, emptying a boxcar from the Iron Range, or loading a refrigerated car bound to somewhere in the immediate distribution area. Working at Fitger's was probably one of the better paying jobs of any industry in Duluth.

The yard foreman at Fitger's was Mr. Lavin, who had started working at the brewery in 1920. His typical workday began at 8:00 A.M. The yardmen would check in with Lavin, whose office was in the basement level of the office building, and he would issue each of them specific tasks to do for the day. Yardmen might be required to fill in for people who were sick, so they needed to be knowledgeable with all facets of the brewery.

The favorite job for the yardmen was to be the truck driver's assistant. In one out of every four places, the bartender would always give them a drink to thank them for delivering the beer. Every Wednesday yardmen loaded two trucks to be delivered to the Superior branch office. One

The bottle house in the mid-1920s, bottling Silver Spray.

truck was filled with kegs (half-barrels) and the other was filled with case beer. They would start loading at 8:00 A.M. and finish around 9:30 A.M., which was beer time. After beer time, the two trucks would journey to the branch office in Superior to unload their goods and pick up empty case beer and kegs from their warehouse. (The Fitger branch office had a total of four employees, two of its own drivers plus a manager and a clerical worker.)

At 8:00 A.M. every day, the local delivery trucks for Duluth would be loaded on the dock at the bottle house. In 1948, there were five trucks—two used strictly for grocery store deliveries, one for grocery stores and off-sale liquor, and the other two for delivering beer to taverns. These trucks were kept clean and painted and always housed in the garage.

Fitger's also had three trucks that were used for transporting cases or anything else from one place to another within the brewery complex. The 1922 chain-drive truck's ignition was a hand crank, which was very dangerous. Fitger's also had a cream-colored panel truck with a musical horn that blared "Roll out the Barrels," a very popular song in its day. A full-time mechanic was employed at Fitger's to keep all of the trucks in good working order.

Railroad cars also needed to be loaded, which was done with only two men. The foreman would go into the boxcar and measure the size of the car. He would then calculate how high to stack the cases to fill the order. Coopen Johnson recalled, "When we finished and actually counted the number of cases, for some reason we'd always be twenty cases short or twenty cases over, so we'd have to modify the car, and that was always a laughing matter."

One of the most unpopular tasks for yardmen was emptying railroad grain cars. The men had to wear masks to avoid inhaling the particulate dust. Johnson explained, "I remember the first time I emptied a grain car. The car was directly under the kettle room. The kettle man at the time, John Gressman, who was over seventy years of age, hollered down to us and told us how to shovel that particulate grain without creating dust. Finally, he came down and showed us. Talking to him later, I asked him about making the beer and I'll always remember him telling me that the beer that they make today was 'belly wash' compared to the beer that was made prior to Prohibition."

One of the later delivery trucks.

REFERENCES

The majority of the information contained within these pages comes directly from Clarence "Coopen" Johnson, former Fitger's employee and unofficial Fitger's historian. Coopen not only had first-hand knowledge of the brewery, but also had access to August Fitger's unpublished business journals and, most importantly, to Mr. Walter Johnson, a Fitger's vice president and plant historian who personally knew August Fitger and Percy Anneke. More information comes from Coopen's interviews with various members of the Fitger and Anneke families, as well as from Fitger's employees Coopen stayed in contact with over the years. Barb Beerhalter also contributed information and research regarding the brewery and the Beerhalters in particular. Further information comes from the following sources:

Books:

Carroll, Francis M. and Franklin R. Raiter. *The Fires of Autumn: The Cloquet–Moose Lake Disaster of 1918*. Minnesota Historical Society Press, St. Paul: 1990.

Van Brunt, Walter, ed. *Duluth and St. Louis County, Minnesota: Their Story and People: An Authentic Narrative of the Past, with Particular Attention to the Modern Era in the Commercial, Industrial, Educational, Civic and Social Development*. American Historical Society: 1921, 3 volumes.

Newspapers:

The Duluth Herald
The Duluth Minnesotian
The Duluth News-Tribune
The Duluth News-Tribune & Herald

ABOUT THE AUTHOR

Clarence "Coopen" Johnson attended Duluth public schools and graduated from Central High School in 1943. Coopen served two years in the U.S. Navy during World War Two aboard the U.S.S. *Gosper*. He graduated from the University of Minnesota Duluth in 1950, where he majored in history. Coopen taught at Esko High School for thirty-two years before retiring in 1984. He also coached Esko High School basketball for eighteen years with a lifetime record of 270 wins and 83 losses and in 1955 brought the first Polar League team to the state tournament, winning the consolation championship.

He taught Duluth history classes at UMD through the University for Seniors program. Coopen worked as a beer distributor for Fitger's for twelve years and served as the company's historian. In June 2003, the Fitger family declared him an "Honorary Fitger" for his knowledge and devotion to the Fitger Brewing Company and the family that founded it. Coopen was a very special person and we enjoyed his friendship throughout the years. Some of our best afternoons were spent listening to him tell of years gone by. He wove such a story, you felt as if you were actually there. We will miss these times and we will dearly miss Coopen. But one thing is certain: We will always remember him and he will always be a part of Fitger's...forever.

Clarence "Coopen" Johnson and his wife, Nancy.

– Scott Vesterstein, September, 2004